ROMEO
AND JULIET

Other books written by Cedric Watts:

Conrad's 'Heart of Darkness': A Critical and Contextual Discussion, 1977
Cunninghame Graham: A Critical Biography (with Laurence Davies), 1979
A Preface to Conrad, 1982
R. B. Cunninghame Graham, 1983
The Deceptive Text: An Introduction to Covert Plots, 1984
A Preface to Keats, 1985
William Shakespeare: 'Measure for Measure', 1986
Hamlet, 1988
Joseph Conrad: A Literary Life, 1989
Joseph Conrad: 'Nostromo', 1990
Literature and Money: Financial Myth and Literary Truth, 1990

Books edited by Cedric Watts:

Joseph Conrad's Letters to R. B. Cunninghame Graham, 1969
The English Novel, 1976
Selected Writings of Cunninghame Graham, 1981
Joseph Conrad: *Lord Jim* (with Robert Hampson), 1986
Joseph Conrad: *'Typhoon' and Other Tales*, 1986
Joseph Conrad: *The Nigger of the 'Narcissus'*, 1988
Joseph Conrad: *'Heart of Darkness' and Other Tales*, 1990

Twayne's New Critical Introductions to Shakespeare

ROMEO AND JULIET

Cedric *Thomas* Watts

Professor of English, University of Sussex

Twayne Publishers, Boston
A Division of G. K. Hall & Co.

Published in the United States by Twayne Publishers
A Division of G. K. Hall & Co.
70 Lincoln Street
Boston, Massachusetts 02111

Published simultaneously in Great Britain by
Harvester Wheatsheaf
66 Wood Lane End, Hemel Hempstead,
Hertfordshire, HP2 4RG
A division of
Simon & Schuster International Group

Twayne's New Critical Introductions to Shakespeare, no. 12

Library of Congress Cataloging-in-Publication Data
Watts, Cedric Thomas.
    Romeo and Juliet / Cedric Watts.
        p.   cm. — (Twayne's new critical introductions to
    Shakespeare ; no. 12)
    Includes bibliographical references and index.
    ISBN 0–8057–8724–0 (hc). — ISBN 0–8057–8725–9 (pbk.)
    1. Shakespeare, William, 1564–1616. Romeo and Juliet.
    I. Title.   II. Series.
    PR2831.W38   1991
    822.3′3—dc20   91–13101
                                                          CIP

Titles in the Series

General Editor's Preface

The *New Critical Introductions to Shakespeare* series will include studies of all Shakespeare's plays, together with two volumes on the non-dramatic verse, and is designed to offer a challenge to all students of Shakespeare.

Each volume will be brief enough to read in an evening, but long enough to avoid those constraints which are inevitable in articles and short essays. Each contributor will develop a sustained critical reading of the play in question, which addresses those difficulties and critical disagreements which each play has generated.

Different plays present different problems, different challenges and excitements. In isolating these, each volume will present a preliminary survey of the play's stage history and critical reception. The volumes then provide a more extended discussion of these matters in the main text, and of matters relating to genre, textual problems and the use of source material, or to historical and theoretical issues. But here, rather than setting a row of dragons at the gate, we have assumed that 'background' should figure only as it emerges into a critical foreground; part of the critical endeavour is to establish, and sift, those issues which seem most pressing.

So, for example, when Shakespeare determined that *his* Othello and Desdemona should have no time to live together, or that Cordelia dies while Hermione survives, his deliberate departures from his source material have a critical significance which is often blurred, when discussed in the context of lengthily detailed surveys of 'the sources'. Alternatively, plays like the *The Merchant of Venice* or *Measure for Measure* show Shakespeare welding together different 'stories' from quite different sources, so that their relation to each other becomes a matter for critical debate. And Shakespeare's dramatic practice poses different critical questions when we ask – or if we ask: few do – why particular characters in a poetic drama speak only in verse or only in prose; or when we try to engage with those recent, dauntingly specialised and controversial textual studies which set out to establish the evidence for authorial revisions or joint authorship. We all read *King Lear* and *Macbeth*, but we are not all textual critics; nor are textual critics always able to show where their arguments have critical consequences which concern us all.

Just as we are not all textual critics, we are not all linguists, cultural anthropologists, psychoanalysts or New Historicists. The diversity of contemporary approaches to Shakespeare is unprecedented, enriching, bewildering. One aim of this series is to represent what is illuminating in this diversity. As the hastiest glance through the list of contributors will confirm, the series does not attempt to 'reread' Shakespeare by placing an ideological grid over the text and reporting on whatever shows through. Nor would the series' contributors always agree with each other's arguments, or premisses; but each has been invited to develop a sustained critical argument which will also provide its own critical and historical context – by taking account of those issues which have perplexed or divided audiences, readers, and critics past and present.

Graham Bradshaw

Contents

Preface

The first two sections of this book, 'The Stage History' and 'The Critical History', illustrate both contrast and complementarity. There is contrast, for the theatrical popularity of *Romeo and Juliet* has been greater than the customary modern critical rating of the work might indicate, and the play has exerted immense cultural influence in its various manifestations on stage, screen and radio, and in musical adaptations. There is complementarity, for some of the critical views naturally influence directors and producers of the work; while the adaptations of, and excisions in, the performed text themselves imply a range of critical judgements about the play's nature and relevance to contemporaneous audiences.

Next, Chapter 1 gives instances of scholarly problems (particularly textual problems) and their critical consequences. Here my aim is to show that *Romeo and Juliet* was originally a rather more protean work than modern editions customarily make clear. The significant differences between the early texts on which all modern editions are based indicate that there is more room for critical and directorial manœuvre than may at first seem to be the case.

Chapter 2 deals with the sources of the play and their adaptation by Shakespeare. One of the purposes of this chapter is to show that Shakespeare's debts extended to the remote past, and that the play gains resonance from some ancient archetypes of myth and legend. Another purpose is to show that though Shakespeare drew materials from numerous previous writers, he was thoroughly original in the verve, articulate intelligence and organisational power with which he transformed those materials.

Chapter 3 discusses aspects of the plot, structure, themes and imagery. Particular attention is given to the many ironies of the work and to the peculiarly intensive organisation of mutually-enhancing contrasts in the play. Chapter 4 is concerned with the characterisation, concentrating on the ways in which the depiction of Romeo and Juliet is related critically to their social environment. Some of the questions raised here are pursued in Chapter 5, which relates the sexual politics of the play to their wider historical and cultural traditions. In its treatment of romantic love and of marriage based on free choice by lovers, *Romeo and Juliet* has been a more fully and influentially political work than has usually been recognised. If the ideal of romantic love has recently encountered widespread scepticism (from Marxists, anthropologists and some feminists, for example), that opposition has itself been anticipated in the text.

In short, the dialectical, paradoxical, contrastive features of *Romeo and Juliet* are those emphasised in this study. The play's lyricism has been justly celebrated; its vivacious intelligence deserves fuller recognition.

Acknowledgements and Editorial Notes

Quotations from *Romeo and Juliet* are, unless otherwise indicated, taken from the Arden text edited by Brian Gibbons (London and New York: Methuen, 1980, reprinted 1983). Quotations from other works of Shakespeare are taken from *The Complete Works: Compact Edition*, edited by Stanley Wells and Gary Taylor (Oxford: OUP, 1988). For copyright permissions, I gratefully acknowledge: Mrs Laura Huxley and Chatto & Windus (for quotations from Aldous Huxley's *Brave New World*); Oxford University Press (C. S. Lewis's *The Allegory of Love* and Germaine Greer's *Shakespeare*); Weidenfeld & Nicolson (Lawrence Stone's *The Family, Sex and Marriage in England 1500–1800*); Secker & Warburg (David Lodge's *Nice Work*); and Methuen & Co. (*Romeo and Juliet*).

In any quotation, a row of three points (. . .) indicates an ellipsis already present in the cited text, whereas a row of five points indicates an omission that I have made. In lines of verse, other than those quoted from the Quartos of *Romeo and Juliet*, I have where necessary inserted a grave accent over any otherwise-unsounded syllable which needs to be sounded in order to preserve the metre. All other emendations to quoted passages are enclosed in square brackets (apart from the citations of the Arden text, in which the square brackets are those supplied by Gibbons). With these exceptions, I have endeavoured to preserve the quoted material unaltered.

I am grateful for the helpful comments of John Glauser and of various colleagues at Sussex University, including Alan Sinfield (who gallantly helped to check the proofs), Jonathan Dollimore, Homi Bhabha and Sybil Oldfield.

The Stage History

A play by Shakespeare moves through time, changing, mutating, breeding, and evolving. Its survival depends on various factors. One factor is the quality of the writing: its intelligence, eloquence, dramatic verve and linguistic complexity. A second factor is the presence of a receptive cultural environment. A third is the readiness of numerous producers, directors, actors, editors, critics and adaptors to modify the text so as to make it congenial to the cultural environment. Sometimes an adaptation, though free, may revitalise aspects of the original; sometimes (by means of textual excisions, perhaps) the play may be changed in tone and pace, and its complexities may be reduced and tamed; and at other times the adaptation may be so extensive that Shakespearian elements survive only vestigially, and the Shakespearian identity perishes. As Shakespeare diversely appropriated and exploited his sources, so he in turn becomes the subject of diverse cultural appropriation and exploitation. He, approving or condoning, would have foreseen such use: Hamlet takes it for granted that a text can be cut or augmented to suit changing circumstances.

In the theatre, some of Shakespeare's plays have 'died' for centuries, because they seemed so alien to prevailing tastes and values. *Troilus and Cressida*, for instance, was probably performed in Shakespeare's day, but the first *proven* British production did not take place until 1907. Since then, it has been performed with steadily increasing frequency, because a variety of cultural changes has made the play's cynicism, scepticism and harshly problematic structure seem perceptively prophetic rather than scandalous and bewildering. Again, *King Lear*, which many twentieth-century critics regarded as the supreme tragedy by Shakespeare, vanished from the English stage for more than a hundred and fifty years: between the 1680s and the 1830s, Shakespeare's play was deemed too harsh, bleak and chaotic; and eighteenth-century audiences preferred Nahum Tate's version, which transformed the play by giving it a happy ending. There Cordelia eventually accepts Edgar's hand in marriage, while Kent, Gloucester and Lear, alive and well, plan a tranquil retirement. After significant early lapses, since 1740 *Romeo and Juliet* has enjoyed relatively steady popularity on stage (second only to *Hamlet*'s, some commentators claim), but that popularity has depended in large part on the readiness of various adaptors to alter, often drastically, both the verse and the plot. The process continues to the present day: there are few productions of *Romeo and Juliet* which do not, by textual omissions or rearrangements, seek to impart fresh 'relevance' to the work. In 1986, for instance, the version directed by Michael Bogdanov cut and rearranged the text for reasons indicated here by Niamh Cusack, who played Juliet:

> Treating the play's last moments as a news conference, with the prologue given by the Duke at the end as a sort of press release, and the reconciliation of the families blatantly posed for the cameras, is to refuse to soften the play, as Shakespeare rather tends to, in its finale. It seems to me to make the play much more real for the audience, something much more like real life. We also cut Friar

Laurence's long recapitulation, again with the idea of not allowing the audience to find comfort in distancing themselves from the situation through a long passage of narrative.[1]

In Shakespeare's day, the earliest printed texts of *Romeo and Juliet* certainly affirmed the play's theatrical popularity. The First Quarto says that it 'hath been often (with great applaufe) plaid publiquely'; and the Second Quarto's claim that 'it hath been fundry times publiquely acted' is repeated in the Third Quarto. (Probably the original actors of Romeo and Juliet were the celebrated Richard Burbage and one Robert Goffe, women's parts being played by boys at that time.) Nevertheless, although there were subsequent performances of versions of the play in Germany in the early seventeenth century, the first fully-documented British performance took place in 1662. The company was Sir William Davenant's, with Henry Harris as Romeo, Thomas Betterton as Mercutio and Mrs Saunderson as Juliet. Samuel Pepys attended the first night and was thoroughly dissatisfied, since the actors had not mastered their lines; and a contemporaneous commentator, John Downes, alleged that Lady Capulet provoked mirth by obscenely mispronouncing '*Count*' (as '*Cunt*') in the phrase 'O my dear *Count!*'. Downes also referred to a version by James Howard in which the play ended happily with both lovers alive, 'fo that when the Tragedy was Reviv'd again 'twas Play'd Alternately, Tragical one Day, and Tragicomical another, for feveral Days together'.[2]

In 1679 Thomas Otway freely adapted the play as *The History and Fall of Caius Marius*, setting the action in ancient Rome, drawing on Plutarch and *Coriolanus*, and combining speeches from *Romeo and Juliet* with much new poetry and plot-material. In his version, the famous speech beginning 'Romeo, Romeo, wherefore art thou Romeo?' opens thus:

O *Marius, Marius!* wherefore art thou *Marius?*
Deny thy Family, renounce thy Name:

> Or if thou wilt not, be but fworn my Love,
> And I'll no longer call *Metellus* Parent.[3]

An influential innovation was Otway's arrangement that
Lavinia (the adaptation's counterpart to Juliet), awakening
after young Marius (Romeo) has taken the poison, should
enjoy a poignant reunion with him before his death. Though
not particularly successful at first, *Caius Marius* was re-
vived in the 1690s and prevailed for the next forty years,
during which it appears to have completely superseded
Shakespeare's play. Otway's use of a Roman political setting
attuned the text to Augustan neoclassicism, and its treatment of civil war gave the play obvious relevance to a society
recovering from the traumas of the English Civil War of the
mid-seventeenth century.

   Romeo and Juliet returned in Theophilus Cibber's production (1744), but Cibber mixed material from Shakespeare's text with lines borrowed from *Two Gentlemen of
Verona* and from Otway's text. Another version, by Thomas
Sheridan, ran successfully in Dublin in 1746. The next
revival was David Garrick's (Drury Lane, 1748): his adaptation, which became more drastic between 1748 and 1750,
proved very popular and, with modification by J. P. Kemble,
endured beyond the mid-nineteenth century. *Romeo and
Juliet* was now established as one of the two or three most
popular of Shakespeare's plays; but Shakespeare would not
have recognised some of its features. Garrick's 1750 text
omitted the references to Rosaline (so that his Romeo is,
from the start, pining for Juliet), increased Juliet's age to
eighteen years, and cut and modified many of the speeches,
seeking to eliminate 'the Jingle and Quibble [i.e. rhyme and
wordplay] which were always thought a great Objection to
performing it'.[4] Like Otway and Cibber, Garrick arranged
for Juliet to awaken before Romeo's death, so that the lovers
could have a final impassioned exchange; and the Prince
was given a new concluding speech emphasising the 'dire
misfortunes' caused by 'private feuds'. To add to the stage
spectacle, Garrick devised for Juliet a funeral procession

with dirge and musical accompaniment. Generally, the main effect of the changes was to reduce the dialectical, contrapuntal verve of the original and to substitute a relatively conventional sentimental love-drama.

In the nineteenth century, the text was heavily revised by the notorious Thomas Bowdler, whose *Family Shakespeare* (completed in 1818) sought to purge the works of all bawdy features; and the acting texts by J. P. Kemble and G. R. French also reflected, in varying degrees, the desire to censor the exuberant sexual frankness of the original. In the 1840s various attempts were nevertheless made, in England and America, to restore much of Shakespeare's play; notably, the American actress Charlotte Cushman largely purged the script of the modifications by Otway, Garrick and Kemble, though the bawdry was still omitted. A remarkable nineteenth-century development was that (in contrast to the Elizabethan custom of assigning female roles to boys) Romeo was repeatedly played by actresses. Charlotte Cushman herself, sturdy and husky-voiced, was widely praised for her fiery performances, the part of Juliet being sometimes taken by her sister, Susan.[5] A previous female Romeo was Ellen Tree; subsequent actresses in the role included Fanny Vining and Ada Swanborough. (Given that Cushman and many other female players also performed as Hamlet, nineteenth-century audiences seem to have adapted readily to the cross-gender convention.) During numerous revivals, including those by Edwin Booth, Henry Irving, Mary Anderson and Maude Adams, the predominantly Shakespearian version of the play gradually regained the stage, though some nineteenth-century productions concluded with Juliet's death and reduced the political aspects of the drama. Both Irving and Beerbohm Tree aimed for historical accuracy in staging by their use of elaborately 'realistic' sets which, at considerable financial expense, gave an opulently pictorial effect to the scenes.

In the twentieth century, revivals of the play multiplied not only in Great Britain but also in the United States, Europe and elsewhere. *Romeo and Juliet* became a standard

classic text for use in schools and universities, so that the
burgeoning of English Literature as a major area of academic
study helped to swell audiences for theatrical productions.
The cinema, radio, television and videos brought *Romeo
and Juliet* to vast audiences; comedy-shows so frequently
burlesqued the orchard scene (on one occasion employing
Frank Bruno, the black heavyweight boxer, as Juliet) that
even people who had never read the play became familiar
with Romeo and Juliet as legendary – if mockable – repre-
sentatives of romantic love. (Tourists in Verona were con-
ducted on pilgrimages to the putative balcony, and in
England the lovers lent incongruous grace to the twenty-
pound banknote.) A celebrated British revival of the stage-
play had taken place in 1935, when (to Peggy Ashcroft's fine
Juliet) Laurence Olivier played Romeo, while John Gielgud, the director, played Mercutio; subsequently in the
same run the men exchanged parts, the relatively lyrical style
of Gielgud contrasting markedly with the virile style of
Olivier. Later, Olivier recalled:

> I've seen, as if you had a coin, the top half John, all
> spiritual, all spirituality, all beauty, all abstract things;
> and myself as all earth, blood, humanity . . . . . I was
> trying to sell realism in Shakespeare.[6]

Among numerous notable subsequent performers as
Romeo were Marius Goring, Eric Portman, Robert Donat,
Alan Badel, John Stride and Mark Rylance; and important,
if controversial, productions included Peter Brook's (Strat-
ford, 1947) and Franco Zeffirelli's (London, 1960, with Judi
Dench as a fervent Juliet). Zeffirelli later made an influential
film version (1968): spectacular, lively and energetic compared with the rather staid Hollywood film by George
Cukor (1936), it was nevertheless criticised as 'a "youth
movie" of the 1960s which glorifies the young and carica-
tures the old';[7] and it mutilated the text with as much
freedom as had the Renato Castellani film (1954), whose
scenic merits nevertheless helped to attract high acclaim at

the Venice Festival. (In the early years of the century, at least eighteen adaptations of *Romeo and Juliet*, including excerpts and burlesques, had appeared on the silent screen.) A BBC Television production, lucid but unadventurous, directed by Alvin Rakoff in 1978, was widely disseminated as a video; and sound recordings on discs and cassettes (among them the Marlowe Dramatic Society version, directed by George Rylands) further propagated the work's influence. As its theme of youthful defiance of the older generation gave the play topicality in the twentieth century, so its bawdy humour, which had embarrassed nineteenth-century editors and producers, increasingly was regarded as an asset instead of a liability. Shakespeare's adroitly paradoxical treatment of love (a treatment now enhancive and idealistic, now reductive and cynical) seemed to gain vindication in the theatre and on screen as cultural attitudes became more liberal. Furthermore, Mercutio's cry 'A plague o' both your houses!' could resonate as a protest 'against the stupidity and cold-hearted cruelty of the old generation who had turned the world, both East and West, into a shambles' (to quote a view of the Prague production in 1963–4).[8] Yet hardly ever was the text performed in its entirety: the modern demand for greater realism entailed hostility to the more stylised passages of verse: ingeniously conceited, punning lines often vanished, while the stylised lamentations in Act 4 Scene 5 were reduced. Thus, though some aspects of the text gained cogent relevance, the challenges offered by conspicuous stylisation tended to be evaded.

After *The Tempest*, *Romeo and Juliet* has probably been the most popular Shakespearian play for operatic adaptation. More than thirty operas have been made of it, ranging from Benda's and Schwanenberger's (both dated 1776) to Zanon's (1969) and Matuszczak's (1970). Gounod's *Roméo et Juliette* (1867) even engendered a parody by Dejazet entitled *Rhum et Eau en Juillet*. Leonard Bernstein's *West Side Story* (1957) translated the plot to modern times and a location in the streets of New York, the feud between noble families becoming a feud between street-gangs. For all the

banality of the lyrics (by Stephen Sondheim), its melodic
and rhythmic facility helped to bring it great commercial
success; and this dance-opera was later filmed by Robert
Wise and Jerome Robbins. The play's capacity to breed and
multiply was well illustrated by a list published in *Shakespeare Quarterly* (vol. 39, no. 5) in 1988.[9] This cited recent
performances of several ballets (music by Tchaikovsky,
Berlioz and Prokofiev; choreography by Richard Ashton,
Amedeo Amodio, Kenneth MacMillan and John Cranko),
revivals of operas (Delius's *A Village Romeo and Juliet*,
based on Gottfried Keller's rustic adaptation, as well as
Gounod's *Roméo et Juliette*), and so many theatrical
productions that for 1987 alone the total was more than
twenty, in locations ranging from Atlanta, Cleveland
(Ohio) and Costa Mesa (California) to Uppsala, Bochum,
Pardubice (Czechoslovakia) and Wellington (New Zea-
land). Five different productions in England in that same
year included even a Spanish translation.

In the sonnets, Shakespeare speaks proudly of his 'eternal
lines'; and in *Julius Caesar*, Cassius cries:

> How many ages hence
> Shall this our lofty scene be acted over,
> In states unborn and accents yet unknown![10]

When we consider the ways in which *Romeo and Juliet*, in
its diverse representations, adaptations and transforma-
tions, has permeated and infiltrated the lives of so many
people over the centuries and around the world, Shakespeare's pride appears prophetic rather than hubristic. This
play has projected through time incalculably influential
images of the idealism and ardour of young lovers who are
mocked, destroyed and yet vindicated by their turbulent
environment; speeches which have become a lodestar of
articulate romanticism; and actions adroitly revealing both
the sexuality of politics and the politics of sexuality. *Romeo
and Juliet* will not last for ever, because nothing ever does;
but by now it has become so protean and multifarious that

its survival for many future generations seems assured. A world in which its diverse voices could no longer re-echo might be so bleak and debased as to be scarcely worth imagining. That world has been prophesied, however, as Chapter 5 will later show.

The Critical History

One difficulty which besets anyone who seeks to write a brief 'critical history' of *Romeo and Juliet* (or of any other play by Shakespeare) is that from the crucial early years too little information has survived, whereas in the last two centuries there is such an immense abundance of information that the survey must be ruthlessly selective. A further consideration is that the distinction between 'stage history' and 'critical history', though traditional and convenient, is false, since every production of the play entails critical evaluation and interpretation. The most practical form of criticism is probably that implicit in the cuts and revisions of the text for performance, whether in the theatre, the cinema or on television.

The earliest evaluative references to *Romeo and Juliet* (notably the title-pages of the earliest texts, the list by Francis Meres, a brief citation in Marston's *The Scourge of Villanie* and the tribute by Leonard Digges near the beginning of the First Folio) tell us little more than that the play was highly popular. The Otway adaptation (*Caius Marius*, 1679) implies a wealth of evaluations; drastic though Otway's plot-changes were, he retained (while reducing their wordplay) versions of the Queen Mab speech, the Nurse's recollections, the orchard scene, the dawn parting (*aubade*), and, indeed, of most of the great 'arias' and 'duets' which would subsequently receive immense critical praise and analysis; so, already, one can infer the establishment of a consensus identifying the most meritorious speeches. Extant explicit and detailed discussion of the work begins only with John Dryden, who in 1684 argued that Shakespeare would have improved the play had he let the 'harmless' Mercutio live on till its end.[1] Samuel Johnson, in 1765, challenged this view, asserting that Mercutio 'has lived out the time allotted him in the construction of the play'. Endorsing Dryden's opposition to 'conceited' (ingeniously witty) verse, Johnson complained that though Shakespeare's comic scenes are 'happily wrought', 'his pathetick strains are always polluted with some unexpected depravations' – 'His persons, however distressed, "have a conceit left them in their misery . . . . .".' Johnson gave special praise to the characterisation of the Nurse, and generally assessed the work as follows:

> This play is one of the most pleasing of our author's performances. The scenes are busy and various, the incidents numerous and important, the catastrophe irresistibly affecting, and the process of the action carried on with such probability . . . . . as tragedy requires.[2]

A less laudatory view was implicit in the popularity of the Garrick–Kemble acting text. By maintaining Otway's innovation, which permitted Romeo and Juliet to have a poignant reunion immediately before their deaths, this reduced the sustained ironic accidentality of the original; by eliminating Romeo's infatuaton with Rosaline, it made him more conventionally sympathetic; and, by its numerous textual excisions, it removed not only many of the conceits to which Johnson objected, and not only much of the bawdry, but also some of the most lyrically imaginative flights; the play became shorter, simpler and more

sentimental. Yet John Potter commented approvingly in
1771–2:

> Mr. *Garrick* found what must be obvious . . . . . , that
> *Shakespeare* had neglected to heighten the Catastrophe to
> so great a degree of distress as it was capable of being
> carried . . . . . Mr. *Garrick* has rendered the whole more
> uniform and regular . . . . .[3]

The Romantic era witnessed a vast surge of 'bardolatry':
Wordsworth, Coleridge, Shelley, Keats, Hazlitt and Lamb
vied in the fervour of their tributes to Shakespeare's genius.
What to Restoration and Augustan tastes had seemed
wayward and irregular in Shakespeare was now frequently
regarded as evidence of the bard's intuitive wisdom and
creative originality. Certainly, among the Augustans, Pope
had declared Shakespeare 'not so much an Imitator, as an
Instrument, of Nature';[4] but this doctrine, enriched by
significant changes in the conception of 'Nature', received
immense amplification in the Romantic period. Coleridge
even resumed the hoary dispute about Mercutio's death to
exemplify the identification:

> Whence [arises] the harmony that strikes us in the wildest
> natural landscapes, ... compared with the visual effect
> from the greater number of artificial plantations? The for-
> mer are effected by a single energy, modified *ab intra* [from
> within] in each component part. Now as this is the parti-
> cular excellence of the Shakespearian dramas generally, so
> is it especially characteristic of the *Romeo and Juliet*.
>   . . . . . [U]pon the death of Mercutio the whole catas-
> trophe depends; it is produced by it. The scene in which it
> occurs serves to show how indifference to every subject
> but one, and aversion to activity on the part of Romeo,
> may be overcome and roused to the most resolute and
> determined conduct. Had not Mercutio been rendered so
> amiable and so interesting, we could not have felt so
> strongly the necessity for Romeo's interference . . . . .[5]

Given the Romantic movement's enthusiasm for intense emotional states and for rebellious individualism, the love-relationship of Romeo and Juliet elicited particularly ardent praise. Hence Hazlitt's expansion of Coleridge's tribute to the play:

> [I]f it has the sweetness of the rose, it has its freshness too; if it has the languor of the nightingale's song, it has also its giddy transport; if it has the softness of a southern spring, it is as glowing and as bright. There is nothing of a sickly and sentimental cast. Romeo and Juliet are in love, but they are not love-sick. Everything speaks the very soul of pleasure, the high and healthy pulse of the passions: the heart beats, the blood circulates and mantles through-out . . . . .
>
> Romeo is Hamlet in love . . . . . He is himself only in his Juliet; she is his only reality, his heart's true home and idol. The rest of the world is to him a passing dream.[6]

Such tributes re-echoed down the nineteenth century; indeed, Sir Walter Raleigh eventually remarked that 'Since the rise of Romantic criticism, the appreciation of Shakespeare has become a kind of auction, where the highest bidder, however extravagant, carries off the prize'.[7] The praise of *Romeo and Juliet*, however, was often qualified. Increasingly the play was seen as an apprentice-piece which lacked the tragic profundity of such later works as *King Lear* or *Macbeth*. Whereas the mature tragedies were taxing and complex in their psychology and ethics, *Romeo and Juliet*, for all its poignancy and vividness, lacked the wide-ranging power to rival them. A. C. Bradley's *Shakespearean Tragedy* (1904) influentially relegated the work:

> *Romeo and Juliet* . . . . . is a pure tragedy, but it is an early work, and in some respects an immature one.
> . . . . . If further we compare the earlier tragedies with the later, we find that it is in the latter, the maturest works, that [the] inward struggle is most emphasised.

. . . . . The love of Romeo and Juliet conducts them to death only because of the senseless hatred of their houses.[8]

A further relegation of the play was advocated by H. B. Charlton in 1949:

It is indeed rich in spells of its own. But as a pattern of the idea of tragedy, it is a failure.

The reasons advanced by Charlton were these. First, Romeo and Juliet are historically unimportant: they lack 'the pomp of historic circumstance' and are 'in effect just a boy and a girl in a novel . . . . . To choose such folk as these for tragic heroes was aesthetically wellnigh an anarchist's gesture.' Secondly, tragedy must have inevitability; and *Romeo and Juliet* lacks inevitability because Shakespeare relies on 'Fate and Fortune' which act by means of the feud between Montagues and Capulets. The feud (Charlton claimed) is inadequate for the purpose, being merely sporadic: for example, Capulet is quite willing to accept Romeo as an uninvited guest at his ball. As for the concepts of 'Fate and Fortune', they were already out of date; being pagan, 'they had faded before the God of the Christians':

Fate was no longer a deity strong enough to carry the responsibility of a tragic universe; at most, it could intervene casually as pure luck, and bad luck as a motive turns tragedy to mere chance . . . . . It fails to provide the indispensable inevitability.

Thus, the play is a failed experiment, and that is why Shakespeare abandoned tragedy for the next few years (1595–9) to concentrate on history and comedy.[9]

Charlton's case was soon challenged by developments in the theatre and in critical theory. The influence of works by Brecht in Germany and by Arthur Miller in the United States helped to call in question the ancient (ultimately

Aristotelian) notion that the protagonists of a tragedy should be of social eminence; and left-wing critics in the 1970s and 1980s were prompt to suggest that the traditional emphasis on tragic 'inevitability' was politically suspect, since it might instil a conservative passivity. Brecht, in contrast, had advocated a drama of which the spectator could say:

> This human being's suffering moves me, because there would have been a way out for him. This is great art: nothing here seems inevitable.[10]

To Brecht, Romeo was a fine study in romantic relativity:

> In Shakespeare he's already in love before he's seen his Juliet at all. After that he's more in love . . . . . Ha, a bursting scrotum! . . . . . It's one of Shakespeare's great realistic strokes to notice that.[11]

Nevertheless, for all the generally increasing critical attention given to Shakespeare's plays during the twentieth century, there was a consolidation of the consensus that *Romeo and Juliet* lacked the power and profundity of the later tragedies. D. A. Traversi, a critic associated with F. R. Leavis and his influential magazine *Scrutiny*, spoke for many when he referred to *Romeo and Juliet* as 'a tragedy at once "literary", artificial, and profoundly sentimental':

> The essentially adolescent passion of Romeo and Juliet, expressed in verse that combines the themes of love and death while drawing freely upon literary convention, appeals a little too consciously to the response of romantic sensationalism. . . . .[12]

So, while *Romeo and Juliet* remained buoyantly popular in the theatre, the critical and scholarly sense of Shakespeare's evolution from the relatively simple and conventional to the relatively complex and profound often tended to marginalise this work as an early and immature experiment. ('It is immature work still', Harley Granville-Barker had declared.)[13] On the other hand, numerous specialised approaches illuminated the linguistic riches of the text. Caroline Spurgeon's pioneering study, *Shakespeare's Imagery and What It Tells Us* (1935), drew attention to the co-ordinating imagery of light (sun, moon, stars, fire, lightning) amid darkness: '. . . . . the beauty and ardour of young love are seen by Shakespeare as the irradiating glory of sunlight and starlight in a dark world.'[14] William Empson's *Seven Types of Ambiguity* engendered a host of ambiguity-seeking literary analysts, and M. M. Mahood's *Shakespeare's Wordplay* (1957) accordingly analysed the play's puns, quibbles and conceits, suggesting that by preserving ambivalence such devices help to ensure that our final emotion is neither 'satisfaction' nor 'dismay' but 'a tragic equilibrium which includes and transcends both these feelings'.[15] This view harmonised quite well with studies of the play's dramatic structure which, like Harry Levin's,[16] stressed its symmetries and counterpoise. Further, the cumulative effect of repeated scrutinies of the play's sources was to heighten the recognition of Shakespeare's power to animate, compress and intensify materials which, when he encountered them, were relatively diffuse and inert.

In the last third of the twentieth century, feminist approaches burgeoned. These displayed considerable divergence. Some critics (notably Lisa Jardine and Kathleen McLuskie) saw Shakespeare as a 'patriarchal bard' who usually maintained demeaning stereotypes of women, while others (Juliet Dusinberre and Germaine Greer, for instance) saw him as progressive in the sense that he shared the Protestant reformers' advocacy of marital love in opposition to the Roman Catholic valuation of the celibate condition.[17] The play could be seen (by Coppélia Kahn) as a condemnation of the self-destructive tendencies of patriarchal society, while Juliet could be commended (by Irene Dash) as a proto-feminist, 'a courageous person attempting to fight for her destiny as a woman'.[18] By giving close consideration to gender relationships, to stereotyping and to patriarchal ideology, feminist approaches imparted new cogency to the text; and similarly, the broad effect of the theoretical developments publicised as 'poststructuralism', 'deconstructionism' or 'cultural materialism' was to question features which previously had often (though not as frequently as their advocates indicated) been taken for granted.[19] Though diverse, these approaches tended to share with Marxism the ambition to extend the recognised territory of the artificial and reduce that of the natural. Ideas of gender, of human identity, and even of reality itself, were all, it was argued, culturally produced: they were variable matters of ideology and discourse, not 'eternal truths'. A fashionable cliché of literary theory in the 1980s was that a text should be seen as 'a site of struggle' in which 'meanings are contested'. Although much of this modish theorising was very ancient in its basis, reviving the Socratic debate about '*physis* versus *nomos*' (nature versus convention) and reinventing Pyrrho's doctrine that 'custom and convention govern human action',[20] it did make some previous approaches seem blinkered and implicitly or unwittingly conservative.

Of course, new blinkers and clichés superseded the old: if critics in the late nineteenth century used confidently and over-confidently terms like 'truth' and 'beauty', their successors a century later talked repetitively of 'modes of discourse' and 'ideological contradictions'. It may appear, indeed, that there are hardly any critical approaches which *Romeo and Juliet*, in its dialectical vigour and brilliantly articulate intelligence, has not critically anticipated. Quotations from the play tend to gleam like multi-faceted diamonds within the grey argumentation of the commentators; and the emotional verve of the play sets standards of vitally poetic eloquence which the critics, trapped in rational prose, may helpfully appraise but can never hope to emulate. A scholarly interpreter may deem *Romeo and Juliet* inferior to Shakespeare's later, 'mature' tragedies; but theatre-goers, who have long preferred that play to *Coriolanus* or *Timon of Athens*, know well the attractions of youthful vitality.

Shakespeare wrote for the theatre, not the lecture-room, and, though he sometimes deemed his career demeaning ('almost thence my nature is subdued / To what it works in, like the dyer's hand'[21]), he would probably have judged the box-office the most empirical test of critical opinion. That test seems to establish *Romeo and Juliet* as one of the half-dozen most successful plays in his huge output.

· 1 ·

Scholarly Problems and Their Critical Implications

THE DATE OF THE PLAY

The earliest printed text of Shakespeare's *Romeo and Juliet* is dated 1597 and states that the play has been frequently and successfully performed by 'the L. of *Hunfdon* his Seruants'.[1] This text was almost certainly printed before the end of March in that year, because, when Lord Hunsdon became Lord Chamberlain on 17 March, Shakespeare's company changed its name to 'The Lord Chamberlain's Men'. The work *may* derive a few details from John Eliot's *Orthoepia Gallica*, which was published in 1593;[2] more significantly, the mimetic realism of several verse speeches (notably the Nurse's, i.iii.16–48, and Capulet's, iii.v.176–95) indicates a technical maturity greater than that of any play prior to 1593. *Romeo and Juliet* appears, then, to have been written between 1593 and 1597, and it is customary to regard the date of writing as 1595. This custom is supported by the work's various similarities to *Love's Labour's Lost*, *A Midsummer Night's Dream* and *Richard II*, which are all believed to have been written in or around 1595. Among

1

these similarities are the verse texture, the lyrical feeling, elements of conceited verbal ingenuity, and details of plot. *Love's Labour's Lost* both celebrates and ironically criticises the aristocratic modes of love, and the current enthusiasm for love-sonnets adulating the lady (an enthusiasm promoted by Sidney's *Astrophil and Stella*) is both indulged and mocked. Berowne's worldly-wise comments on lovers' excesses have some resemblance to Mercutio's, while his urbane eloquence as lover can be related to Romeo's. It is often noted that the burlesque play of 'Pyramus and Thisbe' staged within *A Midsummer Night's Dream* can be regarded as a parody of various features of *Romeo and Juliet*: in each, for example, the deaths of both lovers are a consequence of the man's erroneous belief that the woman has already died. Again, in *A Midsummer Night's Dream*, as in *Romeo and Juliet*, a choleric father wrathfully reproaches a daughter who wishes to choose her own lover instead of accepting the fiancé whom he has selected for her.

The sceptical reader might observe that there is an element of circularity in this dating process. One editor may ascribe *Romeo and Juliet* to 1595 because of its similiarities to *A Midsummer Night's Dream* and *Richard II*, while another editor may ascribe *Richard II* or *A Midsummer Night's Dream* to 1595 because of their similarities (in conceited verse, for instance) to *Romeo and Juliet*. Another consideration is that Shakespeare may have begun a play in one year and put it aside for a while before resuming work on it in a subsequent year; and after its first performance he may well have added further revisions in the light of audience response or the need to adapt the text to varying circumstances (since a play might be performed not only in the open-air theatre but also at court, or before law students, or in a nobleman's mansion). Other things being equal and the contents remaining the same, the earlier the date ascribed to a Shakespeare play, the better that play becomes. Thus, if *Romeo and Juliet* could be proven to have been written in 1593 it would seem somewhat better than if it proved to have been written in early 1596. In the former case, judged by our expectations of

Shakespeare's skills (and our knowledge of his contemporaries' skills) in 1593, *Romeo and Juliet* would seem quite precocious and surprisingly mature; whereas in the latter case its strengths would be relatively unsurprising. The accurate comprehension and evaluation of a literary work depend on accurate knowledge of the work's date of composition. So the element of uncertainty in the case of *Romeo and Juliet* (written *probably* mainly in 1595 but *possibly* in 1593 or 1594 and *just conceivably* in early 1596) slightly blurs the focus of assessment.

When full allowance has been made for that blur, the fact remains that at the time of its appearance, *Romeo and Juliet* was the most brilliant tragedy to have emerged since the ancient Greek drama of Aeschylus, Sophocles and Euripides. It was wholly original in making the central matter the combined fates of two young lovers within a credibly diversified modern society and in telling their story with such acumen and such stylistic verve.

TEXTUAL MATTERS

I recall an incident at a garage. An unusual car drove in; its owner climbed out and patted it proudly. The manager, perplexed by the vehicle's odd appearance, said: 'What make of car is this?' 'It's an Asp', came the reply. 'An *Asp*?', said the manager, still perplexed. 'Yes', responded the owner; 'It's all spare parts; a.s.p.: Asp.'

This man had assembled the car by taking parts from several different makes; having welded them together, he had spray-painted the whole to give it the outward appearance of unity. When we read a Shakespeare play in a standard edition, we are reading a literary Asp. The editor usually welds together parts of the earliest extant texts, adding stage directions, corrections and 'improvements' postulated by previous editors and himself; and the editorial equivalent to the spray-painting is the modernisation and regularisation of spelling, punctuation, typographical conventions, etc., so as to give a uniformly up-to-date appearance to the play.

The text thus becomes easier to read, but we pay a heavy price for such editorial labours. For example, we thus lose the sense of the protean nature of the original, which may have been less like a finished, polished text and more like a 'work in progress' or a pliable body of material for the use of players.

A Quarto is a book made up of sheets of paper each folded twice to form four leaves, and it may therefore have relatively small pages; a Folio is made up of sheets of paper each folded once to form two leaves, and it may have relatively large pages. No manuscript of *Romeo and Juliet* has survived, and the earliest printed text of the play is the First Quarto (alias Q1), dated 1597. It is known as a 'Bad' Quarto. What makes it bad is that it is believed to have been based not on an authoritative manuscript but on a 'memorial reconstruction' by mercenary reporters (if not a single reporter) who were familiar with the stage-play. These reporters, who may well have been actors, wrote down or dictated what they recalled of the work, perhaps consulting some characters' scripts or notes made during performances, and a printer then set in type this 'pirated' version. Given the fallibility of note-takers, memory and handwriting, much of the text became garbled and abbreviated. So this version is relatively short and often unreliable. It cannot, however, be ignored by any modern editor. Some of the gaps in the First Quarto may indicate amnesia by the reporters; but they may indicate that early performances of the play were, at certain points, briefer – either because Shakespeare would later add to the material or because the players had decided to abridge some of the speeches. Again, the First Quarto has various lines and phrases not present in the later printed texts, and even if these are sometimes actors' interpolations, they may still (in some cases) faithfully represent what was said in the theatre. Occasionally the phrasing in Q1 is superior to that in the Second Quarto (Q2); and Q1 sometimes correctly sets as verse what Q2 sets as prose. Furthermore, as we might expect in a text reported by men involved in actual productions, the stage directions in Q1 are often fuller and more informative than those in other printed texts of the play. For instance (using act, scene and line references of the Arden edition): iii.i.89 has '*Tibalt vnder Romeos arme thruſts Mercutio in, and flyes.*'; iii.iii.107 has '*He offers to ſtab himſelfe, and Nurſe ſnatches the dagger away.*'; iv.v.50 has '*All at once cry out and wring their hands.*'; and iv.v.95 has '*They all but the Nurſe goe foorth, caſting Roſemary on her and ſhutting the Curtens.*'.[3] Some of them (like the last of these four examples) may be stopgaps, substitutes for forgotten dialogue; but others may well be accurate recollections of the stage business.

The Second Quarto, dated 1599, is considerably longer than Q1 (3,007 lines as against Q1's 2,232), and, in the main, is superior in quality. It is deemed by numerous editors to have been printed from 'foul papers': that is, from a draft by Shakespeare bearing various additions and revisions. Sometimes, however, the printer used Q1 as copy, perhaps because the manuscript was unclear. (Another and less persuasive theory is that Q2 was based on a copy of Q1 which had been corrected and augmented by a scribe who had consulted the manuscript.) Signs of Shakespeare's presence in Q2 include the stage-direction '*Enter Will Kemp*' (instead of '*Enter Peter*') at what is now iv.v.102, Will Kemp being the name of the comic actor who was to play the role. Some lines in Q2 are garbled because the printer has set in type Shakespeare's first and second thoughts, as though the author, writing in haste, had failed to cross out the original phrases.

There were several subsequent Quarto texts, but all are thought to derive from Q2, as does (via Q3) the first Folio text of the play. (These subsequent texts still contain their own variants: thus, the First Folio version omits the entire Prologue.) Modern editors, therefore, tend to rely heavily on Q2 while incorporating elements of Q1. Both texts lack Act and Scene divisions and some necessary stage-directions; these, and various emendations, are supplied by the editors. Scholarship implies evaluation: an editor of Shakespeare, when constructing a new text from the early materials, is usually influenced by the criteria of coherence, intelligibility

and quality: so, if Q1's version of a speech seems superior
in quality to Q2's, Q1's may be preferred by him even if
Q2 is generally thought to be more authoritative. (Small
emendations may also be selected from the wide range of
texts and editions between Q2 and the present day.)

To illustrate some differences between Q1 and Q2, and
to show how greatly our sense of the nature of the text
may be influenced by modern editorial procedures, I cite the
speeches which are now located at the end of Act 2, Scene 2,
and at the beginning of Act 2, Scene 3. First, here is the
version offered by Q1:

> *Ro:* Would I were thy bird.
> *Iul:* Sweet fo would I,
> Yet I fhould kill thee with much cherrifhing thee.
> Good night, good night, parting is fuch fweet forrow,
> That I fhall fay good night till it be morrow.   (breaft,
> *Rom:* Sleepe dwell vpon thine eyes, peace on thy
> I would that I were fleep and peace of fweet to reft.
> Now will I to my Ghoftly fathers Cell,
> His help to craue, and my good hap to tell.
>
>   *Enter Frier Francis.*   (night,
> *Frier:* The gray ey'd morne fmiles on the frowning
> Checkring the Eafterne clouds with ftreakes of light,
> And flecked darkenes like a drunkard reeles,
> From forth daies path, and *Titans* fierie wheeles:
> Now ere the Sunne aduance his burning eye,
> The world to cheare, and nights darke dew to drie,
> We muft vp fill this oafier Cage of ours,
> With balefull weeds, and precious iuyced flowers,

Next, here is the version offered by Q2:

> *Ro.* I would I were thy bird.
> *Iu.* Sweete fo would I,
> Yet I fhould kill thee with much cherifhing:
> Good night, good night.

Parting is ſuch ſweete ſorrow,
That I ſhall ſay good night, till it be morrow.
   Iu. Sleep dwel vpon thine eyes, peace in thy breaſt.
   Ro. Would I were ſleepe and peace ſo ſweet to reſt
The grey eyde morne ſmiles on the frowning night,
Checkring the Eaſterne Clouds with ſtreaks of light
And darkneſſe fleckted like a drunkard reels,
From forth daies pathway, made by *Tytans* wheeles.
Hence will I to my ghoſtly Friers cloſe cell,
His helpe to craue, and my deare hap to tell.
                                 Exit.

        Enter Frier alone with a basket.   (night,
   Fri. The grey-eyed morne ſmiles on the frowning
Checking the Eaſterne clowdes with ſtreaks of light:
And fleckeld darkneſſe like a drunkard reeles,
From forth daies path, and *Titans* burning wheels:
Now ere the ſun aduance his burning eie,
The day to cheere, and nights dancke dewe to drie,
I muſt vpfull this oſier cage of ours,
With balefull weedes, and precious iuyced flowers,

Finally, the version offered by a modern edition, the Arden
text published in 1980. (Here the square brackets are those
furnished in that text:)

Romeo. I would I were thy bird.
Juliet.   Sweet, so would I:
   Yet I should kill thee with much cherishing.
   Good night, good night. Parting is such sweet sorrow
   That I shall say good night till it be morrow.   185
                                [Exit Juliet.]
Romeo. Sleep dwell upon thine eyes, peace in thy breast.
   Would I were sleep and peace so sweet to rest.
   The grey-ey'd morn smiles on the frowning night,
   Chequering the eastern clouds with streaks of light;
   And darkness fleckled like a drunkard reels   190
   From forth day's pathway, made by Titan's wheels.

Hence will I to my ghostly Sire's close cell,
His help to crave and my dear hap to tell.   *Exit.*

[SCENE III]
Enter FRIAR [LAURENCE] *alone with a basket.*

Friar L. Now, ere the sun advance his burning eye
The day to cheer, and night's dank dew to dry,
I must upfill this osier cage of ours
With baleful weeds and precious-juicèd flowers.

The reader will notice that although editors are convinced
that Q2 is, in general, superior to and more authoritative
than Q1, this modern edition not only follows Q1's arrangement of the lines now numbered 184–5 (which is more
accurate in its rendering of the iambic pentameter) but also
endorses Q1's ascription of line 186 to Romeo rather than
to Juliet. Again, Q2 is clearly faulty in ascribing both to
Romeo and the Friar the four lines (now numbered 188–191)
describing the dawn. Evidently Shakespeare revised them,
and the printer of Q2 erroneously set in type both the
earlier version and the revised version; scholars subsequently
wrangle about which is which. Whether the lines should
finally be ascribed to Romeo rather than to the Friar is
mainly a matter of critical judgement; the Arden editor has
decided that 'the lines are characteristic of Romeo rather
than the uninventive personifications of the Friar'.[4] It could,
however, be argued that since both Q1 and Q2 give these
lines to the Friar, and since Q2's additional ascription of
them to Romeo may be a mistaken allocation of the revised
lines written in the margin, the Friar should be allowed these
few moments of inventiveness. Furthermore, if the passage
is given to Romeo, the transition from line 187 to 188 is
rather abrupt, particularly as he has good reason to think
of this rapturous night as 'smiling' rather than 'frowning';
whereas, if they are given to the Friar, these four lines about
daybreak blend naturally with the following couplet about

dew at dawn. So, although the Arden text ascribes them to Romeo's speech at the end of Scene 2, other modern editions (for example, the Cambridge text, 1969, and *The Riverside Shakespeare*, 1974) ascribe them to the Friar's speech at the beginning of Scene 3. Here an ostensibly scholarly matter is clearly also a critical matter depending on, and affecting, judgements of character and pace. Incidentally, an instance of the aesthetic judgement's power to overrule the textual evidence is provided by the phrase 'ghostly Sire's' (line 192), which the Arden editor has preferred to the phrasing proffered by Q1 and Q2 ('Ghostly fathers' and 'ghostly Friers' respectively), even though their phrasing makes quite satisfactory sense.

There are occasions when the early and the modern texts may all be wrong. For example, at what is now III.ii.5–7, Juliet says in Q2:

Spread thy cloſe curtaine loue-performing night,
That runnawayes eyes may wincke, and *Romeo*
Leape to theſe armes, vntalkt of and vnſeene. . . . .

Q1 has no equivalent lines at all. The Arden edition gives:

Spread thy close curtain, love-performing night,
That runaway's eyes may wink, and Romeo
Leap to these arms untalk'd-of and unseen.

The problematic word here is 'runaway's'. In the first place, this word, being trisyllabic, is metrically awkward; a disyllabic would be more appropriate. Secondly, much strained ingenuity is required to make sense of it: who or what is the 'runaway'? Editors implausibly suggest 'the night' and 'the sun', or, reading the noun as 'runaways', 'the horses of the sun' and 'vagrant night wanderers'. I think it possible that the printer of Q2 erroneously saw as 'runawaies' (and set as 'runnawayes') a word which in the manuscript was 'rumoures', and that the correct modern version of the line should be: 'That Rumour's eyes may wink, and Romeo'.[5]

('Wink' means simply 'close'.) Pictures showing the personification of Rumour often showed a figure with many
tongues and eyes; in literature, clandestine lovers traditionally fear betrayal by prying eyes and gossips' rumours. Ben
Jonson's *Volpone* gives a translation of an ode by Catullus
which includes these lines:

> Why should we defer our joys?
> Fame and rumour are but toys.
> Cannot we delude the eyes
> Of a few poor household spies?[6]

The Prologue to Shakespeare's *Henry IV, Part Two* is
spoken by '*Rumour . . . . . painted full of tongues*', and he
associates his journey with rapid movement from east to
west; so Shakespeare may have been influenced there by
Juliet's association of Rumour with a desire that the horses
of the sun should speed westward. 'Rumour's' not only fits
the metre far better than does 'runaway's'; it also alliterates
more fully with 'Romeo'; and, above all, it leads naturally
to the subsequent line's hope that if the lovers are concealed
by darkness, their embrace may be 'untalk'd of'.

The modern text's phrase 'runaway's eyes' is just one
problematic phrase among many in *Romeo and Juliet*. We
thus see that the play is textually more protean, variable and
flexible than we may at first have supposed: a fact which
may give interpreters more freedom. Yet, given that a single
phrase may provide the keynote of a whole critical interpretation, interpreters may also need caution. A particularly
important consideration is that neither Q1 nor Q2 has any
explicit Act or Scene divisions; and the arbitrariness of some
of the divisions imposed by subsequent editors is shown by
the way in which the first line in what is now Act 2, Scene 2
completes a rhyming couplet begun by the last line of what
is now Act 2, Scene 1. A natural unity has been artificially
severed. The original staging of the play was, evidently,
more fluently rapid than the now-customary divisions of
Act and Scene suggest.

In short, the most honest modern edition of *Romeo and Juliet* might be one which contained both the First Quarto text, reproduced word for word and comma for comma, warts and all, and the Second Quarto text, similarly reproduced in its original state; and the reader would then be invited to construct in imagination his or her own modern version in the light of that information. Such an edition might at first seem daunting; but it would be honest in its representation, without alteration, of the earliest extant materials of the play; and, by making clear the immense variety of alternatives presented by the textual divergencies, it might be liberating for future critics, directors and actors. We would be reminded that the play may well have been performed with considerable variation in Shakespeare's own time. If a modern director wishes to cut or adapt the text, there is Shakespearian warrant for such a practice. In *Hamlet*, when Polonius complains that the First Player's recitation about Pyrrhus is too long, Hamlet promptly replies: 'It shall to the barber's, with your beard.' Again, when Hamlet asks the Players to stage 'The Murder of Gonzago' at court, he asks them to add to its text 'a speech of some dozen or sixteen lines' which he himself has written; so Shakespeare was familiar with the practice of modifying a play to give it fresh contemporaneity.[7] So, if we see *Romeo and Juliet* in its relatively pristine form, that of the Quartos, their variants and their archaic features not only remind us of the historical and cultural circumstances in which the work was engendered; they also remind us that it was a play which evidently changed and developed as it moved through time, and may properly continue to change and develop in its continuing theatrical manifestations.

In this book, it would be impractical for me to use the Quartos as the basic texts for citation, since it would be difficult for the present readers to consult such texts for themselves; a difficulty compounded by the absence of Act and Scene divisions. So, for practicality's sake, I have generally used the current Arden edition, which (at the time of writing) is widely available in bookshops and libraries. I hope, however, that the textual comparisons made in this section will forewarn the reader that the passages which are subsequently quoted may not always correspond precisely to what Shakespeare intended, and that *Romeo and Juliet*, in Shakespeare's day, may well have varied quite significantly, over the years, in particular performances at different locations. The play probably possessed more 'play' (flexibility, adaptability) than we can now discern.

· 2 ·

The Sources and Their Adaptation

PREAMBLE

There were various kinds of source-material for a Shakespeare play. Often he adapted an available story or chronicle, which in turn might have had numerous analogues and antecedents. Many prior literary texts contributed or suggested to him thematic, structural, psychological and technical possibilities. He could draw on situations and relationships explored in his own previous works. Personal experience, of the kinds transmuted as his sonnet sequence, made their own multifarious contributions.

Tracing narrative sources of *Romeo and Juliet* may at first appear to be a pedantic exercise, a labour of literary archaeology. In reality, this is a critically crucial activity. By comparing Shakespeare's version with its antecedents, we are able, by noting his changes to the source-matter, to define his imaginative intentions; and this, in turn, enables us to adjudicate between rival interpretations. In the case of *King Lear*, for example, we know that in all the extant sources, the story of Lear ends relatively happily, with Lear restored to his throne and dying eventually in peaceful old age, outlived by Cordelia. Only in Shakespeare's play does the story end with harrowing bleakness, the murder of Cordelia precipitating the sudden death of the aged king. The harsh and bleak termination seems to be Shakespeare's distinctive contribution: and this clearly strengthens the claims of atheistic or antitheistic interpreters of the play who seek to combat Christian interpretations. Again, if we observe how *Macbeth* alters the data of Holinshed's *Chronicles* so as to make Macbeth more culpable, Duncan and Banquo relatively innocent, and the Weird Sisters more repulsive, we infer that Shakespeare has endeavoured to flatter the new monarch, King James I, descendant of Banquo and author of *Daemonologie*.

Comparisons with his source-materials can also be a way of vindicating Shakespeare's high reputation. From time to time, predictably, that reputation is challenged. In the 1980s and 1990s various critics, notably Alan Sinfield and Gary Taylor,[1] argued that Shakespeare's reputation had been maintained by cultural conservatism and that the bard should be toppled from his eminence. Such challenges are quite proper in principle, since literary reputations are constantly being reappraised as cultural changes proceed. There are various modes of response; one of the relatively objective modes is to compare a Shakespeare play with its sources. Then a common discovery is that from apparently unpromising or limited material Shakespeare has made a drama of unprecedented eloquence, intensity and intelligence. Cinthio's story of Disdemona and the Moor reads not like a tragedy but rather like a naïve narrative of sordid crime; Shakespeare's *Othello* has transmuted a tawdry yarn into a powerful, intense and richly problematic tragedy. A similar sense of Shakespeare's power to transmute base metals into gold is evoked if we consider the transmission of the story of Romeo and Juliet.

THE STORY'S HISTORY

In *Romeo and Juliet*, Juliet is thought dead, is mourned and is entombed in a dank subterranean vault; but she is not truly dead, and reawakens. This detail of the plot could be traced back, via poems, prose romances and ancient classical legends, to the very earliest origins of the tragic tradition: the religious motif of the nature-representative who apparently dies but is resurrected. Aristotle claimed, in the fifth century BC, that tragedy developed from the dithyramb, the hymn sung in honour of Dionysus, god of the vine, who could be destroyed and yet could live again.[2] Many ancient myths (Demeter and Persephone, Orpheus and Eurydice, Admetus and Alcestis) have their resurrection motifs; and, as Sir James Frazer's *The Golden Bough* pointed out in the nineteenth century, all of them have a clear material basis: they celebrate the seasonal cycle; they stem from recognition that in winter nature appears to die, but in spring it revives.[3] If tragedy emphasises suffering and loss, comedy emphasises revival and restoration; and, in his late romances (*Pericles*, *Cymbeline*, *The Winter's Tale* and *The Tempest*), Shakespeare would endeavour to fuse both.

In the second century AD, the *Ephesiaca* by Xenophon of Ephesus tells how two teenagers, Anthia and Habrocomes, fall in love at first sight and subsequently marry. Anthia becomes separated from her husband and is rescued from robbers by one Perilaus, who himself then seeks to marry her. To evade this second marriage, Anthia bribes a needy physician to supply her with a potion to enable her to commit suicide; but he, scrupulously, supplies not a poison but a soporific. On her bridal day she drinks it, swoons, is thought dead and is interred in a tomb; later, she awakens there and is carried away by tomb-robbers. Habrocomes learns of Anthia's apparent death and interment, and hastens to the tomb; after many vicissitudes he and Anthia are at last reunited.

There is a consensus among commentators that Shakespeare had no direct knowledge of the *Ephesiaca*; what is evident is that it represents an intermediate stage between

those ancient resurrection myths and the subsequent tales
which were studied by Shakespeare. Xenophon helped to
transmit the 'apparent death' or *Scheintod* motif (already
established in legends like those of Eurydice and Alcestis) as
well as the interlinked motifs of 'death as lover, tomb as
bridal chamber' which had appeared in Sophocles' *Anti-
gone*, Petronius' *Satyricon*, Apuleius' *Metamorphoses*,
Achilles Tatius' *Leucippe and Clitophon* and Heliodorus'
Ethiopian Story, and which modern opera-lovers encounter
in Verdi's *Aïda*.

By the fifteenth century, the plot had already accumulated
more of the features now familiar to us. The *Cinquante Nov-
elle* of Masuccio Salernitano (Naples, 1476), includes the
story of Mariotto and Giannozza of Siena. These two lovers
are secretly married by a Friar. Mariotto then quarrels with
a citizen, kills him, and is banished. Giannozza's irascible
father urges her to marry a suitor he has chosen; so, after
sending a message to forewarn her husband of her plan, she
takes a sleeping potion provided by the Friar, is thought dead
and is entombed. The Friar releases her, and she sails to Alex-
andria in the hope of meeting Mariotto there. But her message
has not reached him, for the messenger has been captured by
pirates. Hearing that she has died, Mariotto returns home
and, while attempting to open the tomb, is arrested. He is
beheaded, and Giannozza consequently dies of grief.

A subsequent version by Luigi da Porto transfers the
events to Verona, renames the lovers 'Romeo' and 'Giulietta', specifies a feud between their two families (the Montecchi and the Cappelletti), and says that Romeo met Giulietta
when he went to a ball in the hope of seeing a lady who had
repulsed his courtship. After the clandestine marriage to
Giulietta, which Friar Lorenzo hopes will unite the feuding
families, Romeo kills one Thebaldo and flees to Mantua.
Giulietta takes the sleeping potion to avoid marriage to
a suitor, a count, who is favoured by her father. Friar
Lorenzo's message to Romeo is entrusted to another Friar
who fails to deliver it, as Romeo is absent. Romeo, mean-
while, hearing that she is dead, has gone to the tomb and

taken poison; Giulietta awakens, speaks with him and embraces him; he dies; and she commits suicide – by holding her breath! The parents, on learning of the circumstances, are reconciled, and the feud ends.[4]

The tale was then transmitted and elaborated by Bandello, Boaistuau and various adaptors, acquiring a conspiratorial nurse, a culpable apothecary, and other familiar features. Eventually it became Arthur Brooke's long narrative poem, *The Tragicall Historye of Romeus and Juliet* (1562), and this was Shakespeare's main source. (The poem is available in Geoffrey Bullough's *Narrative and Dramatic Sources of Shakespeare*, Vol. I, and – in an abridged version – in the Arden *Romeo and Juliet* edited by Brian Gibbons.)

Brooke's account is pedestrian, prolix, and rather naïve. The versification is the shuffling jog-trot of 'Poulter's Measure': lines with, alternately, twelve syllables (six stresses: iambic hexameter) and fourteen syllables (seven stresses: iambic heptameter), though they have many irregularities; all too often, the reader has to tackle a line twice to identify its central caesura so that the stresses can then be arranged on either side of it. To make a just comparison (where Brooke's text is very close to Shakespeare's): here is how Brooke presents the anger of Juliet's father when she declines Paris:

> Onlesse by Wensday next, thou bende as I am bent,
> And at our castle cald Free towne, thou freely doe assent
> To Counte Paris sute, and promise to agree
> To whatsoever then shall passe, twixt him, my wife, and
> me,
> Not onely will I geve all that I have away
> From thee, to those that shall me love, me honor, and
> obay,
> But also too so close, and to so hard a gaole,
> I shall thee wed, for all thy life, that sure thou shalt not
> fayle
> A thousand times a day to wishe for sodayn death,
> And curse the day, and howre when first thy lunges did
> geve thee breath.

> Advise thee well, and say that thou art warnèd now,
> And thinke not that I speake in sport, or mynd to break
>   my vowe.[5]

Here is a counterpart speech in the play (III.v.176–89):

> God's bread, it makes me mad! Day, night, work, play,
> Alone, in company, still my care hath been
> To have her match'd. And having now provided
> A gentleman of noble parentage,
> Of fair demesnes, youthful and nobly lign'd,
> Stuff'd, as they say, with honourable parts,
> Proportion'd as one's thought would wish a man –
> And then to have a wretched puling fool,
> A whining mammet, in her fortune's tender,
> To answer, 'I'll not wed, I cannot love,.
> I am too young, I pray you pardon me!'
> But, and you will not wed, I'll pardon you!
> Graze where you will, you shall not house with me.
> Look to't, think on't, I do not use to jest.

The spelling and punctuation have been editorially mod-
ernised to a far greater extent in the latter passage than in the
former; but, when allowance has been made for this, it is
obvious that Shakespeare's version is altogether more vivid
and expressive of character than is Brooke's. Whereas the
Poulter's Measure, awkward and halting, obtrudes itself like
an unreliable metronome between reader and imaginary
speaker, Shakespeare's blank verse is relatively transparent;
the metre is both firm and supple, blending easily with the
colloquial impetuosity of Capulet's diction. The rhythms
and syntax readily create the illusion of the spontaneous
utterance of an exasperated parent voicing righteous indignation with hardly-controlled violence. In general, Brooke's
predominantly naïve style throws into relief, by contrast,
the linguistic virtuosity of Shakespeare's text: the keen
lyricism, sententious gravity, colloquial vitality and idioma-
tic ease.

In converting the narrative into a play, Shakespeare has given direct physicality, movement, colour, vitality and a diversity of modes of eloquence in poetry and prose to what formerly was relatively inert: everywhere there is new life, intelligence and questing cogency. Contrasts in discourse, characterisation, tone and scene are repeatedly introduced or accentuated. In Brooke, the time-scale of events is vague but lengthy: at least nine months elapse. In Shakespeare, the time-scale is dramatically compressed to just four days (from Sunday to Thursday morning), so that the momentum is impetuously rapid. Furthermore, this momentum is given thematic force, for one of the main themes then becomes the attraction and danger of impetuous action. The love-relationship gains the intensity and poignancy of precipitate brevity. And Shakespeare not only enlivens the structure but also co-ordinates it very systematically. Brooke's poem began with a sonnet summarising the plot; Shakespeare places a summarising sonnet at the beginning not only of Act 1 but also of Act 2, and (with superbly symbolic use of poetic form) lets the first exchange of Romeo and Juliet blend into a formally perfect sonnet. In Brooke the feud is presented with relative vagueness as a matter in the background of the main action until the killing which leads to Romeus's banishment; Shakespeare boldly foregrounds the feud first at the outset, second near the midpoint (Act 3 Scene 1, after which the Prince banishes Romeo), and third at the conclusion, so that the contrast between the private and the public, the intimate and the political, becomes much more prominent and forceful. The play's profusion of minor characters (Abram, Balthasar, Peter, Sampson, Gregory, Potpan, Anthony, etc.) also helps to establish as significant realities the social and political contexts.

Brooke introduced Paris and Tybalt at a relatively late stage in the action, when his plot required their prominent presence; Shakespeare introduces them early on. This change not only gives greater coherence to the action; it engenders suspense and cruel ironies, and enhances the

variety by adding to the arrangement of mutually-
emphasising contrasted figures. Paris becomes prominent as
a noble, civilised and unwitting rival to Romeo; it is
Shakespeare who adds the scenes in which he encounters
Juliet at Laurence's cell, and eventually, in mourning,
clashes with Romeo at the monument and is there slain; in
Brooke he had outlived the lovers. Shakespeare not only
augments the dramatic violence of the concluding events; he
also compounds the sense of cruel fatality, whereby well-
meant endeavours lead to destruction. Paris is the Prince's
kinsman and an ally of the Capulets; so his death serves to
increase the sense of waste entailed by the feud and gives
greater moral force to the reconciliation. As a conventional
though sincerely affectionate wooer of Juliet, Paris helps the
dramatisation of the claims of the traditional arranged
marriage and rational wooing, in contrast to the passionate
imperatives and the epiphanic sexuality of the love-match.
Again, by establishing early in the action the implacable
ruthlessness of Tybalt (now much more strongly characterised than in Brooke), Shakespeare increases suspense and
amplifies the contrast between impetuous hate and impetuous love.

Mercutio, mercurially lively and dynamic as a characterisation, is predominantly Shakespeare's creation; Brooke's
Mercutio makes only a very brief appearance as one who, at
the Capulet's ball, holds Juliet's hand for a while. Shakespeare's Mercutio is unique yet immediately recognisable as a
familiar type: the self-aware, entertainingly sceptical young
man who is as agile in body as in wit, who delights in a self-
displaying mockery of tradition and convention, contrasting with the slower and more pacific Benvolio and the
amorously preoccupied Romeo. In his death, he condemns
the feud for which he dies; but his death, in turn, provokes
Romeo's slaying of Tybalt, leading to the banishment and
the final disaster.

In the case of the Nurse, the poem had provided a substantial base for the characterisation, for already there she
was verbose, prattling, teasing, crafty and vulgarly reminis-

cential. When describing the infant Juliet to Romeo, for instance, she says:

> A thousand times and more I laid her on my lappe,
> And clapt her on the buttocke soft and kist where I did
>   clappe
> And gladder then was I of such a kisse forsooth,
> Then I had been to have a kisse of some olde lechers
>   mouth.[6]

Shakespeare has seized and developed such tones, so that his Nurse, though more vocal and active than Brooke's, is very similar as an affectionate yet wily pragmatist who, consistently inconsistent, will praise first Paris, then Romeo, then Paris again, each time hoping to ingratiate herself further with the family in which she is more an honorary aunt than a servant. Other characters have a similarly strong basis in Brooke's pages: Capulet's shift from being a considerate father to a domineering one was already delineated there; the benevolent old Friar (Lorenzo in Brooke, Laurence in Shakespeare) and even the needy apothecary (eventually hanged in the poem, though not in the play) had been substantially presented. Romeo becomes rather more vigorous and ardent, yet also more troubled by foreboding, in Shakespeare's handling. Juliet becomes younger in years (thirteen instead of sixteen) yet more intense, somewhat less deceitful, more intelligently vivacious; initially deferential yet capable of maturing rapidly towards the determination to choose her own destiny.

As a thematic basis and metaphysical co-ordinator of his tale, Brooke had repeatedly emphasised the dominance of Fortune, regarded as the fickle deity of chance and change. In Shakespeare, 'Fortune' and 'the stars' are invoked (though less frequently than in Brooke) as forces hostile to the lovers; this metaphysic is not pedantically expounded, as it had been in the poem, so it remains relatively unfocused, looser, more ambiguous and less archaic; and the references to the malign stars form part of the network of images of light amid darkness. An even more important shift occurs in the treatment of the lovers. Heirs of the deconstructionists (those literary theorists who in the 1970s and 1980s emphasised and exaggerated the value of detecting contradictions within texts) should be delighted by the fact that Brooke's preface is contradicted by the tenor of his narrative. The dismally moralistic and anti-Catholicist preface ('To the Reader') says:

> The glorious triumphe of the continent man upon the lustes of wanton fleshe, incourageth men to honest restraynt of wyld affections, the shameful and wretched endes of such, as have yelded their libertie thrall to fowle desires, teache men to witholde them selves from the hedlong fall of loose dishonestie . . . . . And to this ende (good Reader) is this tragicall matter written, to describe unto thee a coople of unfortunate lovers, thralling themselves to unhonest desire, neglecting the authoritie and advise of parents and frendes, conferring their principall counsels with dronken gossyppes, and superstitious friers (the naturally fitte instrumentes of unchastitie) attemptyng all adventures of peryll, for thattaynyng of their wished lust, usyng auriculer confession (the kay of whoredome, and treason) for furtheraunce of theyr purpose, abusyng the honorable name of lawefull mariage, the cloke the shame of stolne contractes, finallye, by all meanes of unhonest lyfe, hastyng to most unhappye deathe . . . . .[7]

In his narrative, however, Brooke represents with great sympathy not only Romeus and Juliet but also the Friar, and says finally that the reconciled Montagewes and Capelets erected a stately tomb,

> lest that length of time might from our myndes remove
> The memory of so perfect, sound, and so approvèd
>   love. . . . .

The main reason for this marked discrepancy is, probably,

that Brooke added the speciously puritanical preface in the hope of averting moral condemnation of his story. His terms indicate that there was a widespread conflict between the notion that lovers should be governed by 'the authoritie and advise of parents and frendes' and the notion that lovers should be governed by their own private desires and wishes. Shakespeare's Prologue, in contrast, makes clear from the outset that the dramatist expects our sympathies to lie strongly with the 'star-cross'd lovers' who experience 'misadventur'd piteous overthrows'. But the greater prominence given in the play to the courtship by Paris and its approval by Juliet's parents, and the deliberate interweaving of Paris's tragic fate with Romeo's, does give a full dialectical presentation of the case for, as well as against, the traditional arranged match. What had existed as unresolved contradiction in the contrast between Brooke's preface and story becomes a cogently structured and resolved debate within Shakespeare's drama.

While Shakespeare moderates Brooke's heavy insistence on the turning of fickle Fortune's wheel, he introduces a network of ironic themes and lyrical leitmotifs. Among the ironic themes is that of 'impeded communication': the play provides at least five instances of messages going astray or being impeded by accident or design. The leitmotifs, as Brian Gibbons remarks,

> creat[e] a sense of deep inner coherence in the action to which the characters testify, as if by subconscious prompting – as when Romeo and Juliet speak of stars, lightning, torches and rich jewels in darkness, or when Capulet compares Verona's youth to buds and flowers and their fathers to limping winter, or when Romeo compares himself to a mariner risking shipwreck, or when the Friar observes 'The earth that's nature's mother is her tomb'. The intensive and recurrent use of a group of leitmotivs gives a distinctively sharp lyric quality to the tragedy.[8]

But, in addition to the lyrical imagery, Shakespeare offers a diversity of bawdy allusions. Brooke's version chastely eschews 'indecent' wit; Shakespeare revels in it, so that even a clock becomes randy – 'the bawdy hand of the dial is now upon the prick of noon'. Sampson, Gregory, Mercutio and the Nurse all relish jests about fornication: thus they provide the salt and vinegar to offset the sweetness of the play's lyricism. Above all, they show that Shakespeare had a strongly dialectical imagination: he constantly imagines critical contrasts. The ardently idealistic love of Romeo and Juliet criticises, and yet is implicitly questioned by, the profusion of references to love as mere comical or aggressive carnality. Once again, the comparison with Brooke emphasises Shakespeare's searchingly creative genius: his questing, testing intelligence which, during a taut, contrastive, and splendidly varied action, explores and exploits tensions within the ideological definitions of human nature.

· 3 ·

Title, Structure and Themes

THE TITLE AND SHAKESPEARE'S
TRAGEDIES OF LOVERS

The First Quarto entitled the play 'An excellent conceited Tragedie of Romeo and Iuliet' (i.e. 'An excellent imaginative Tragedy. . . . .' or 'An excellently imagined Tragedy. . . . .'). The Second Quarto entitled it 'The most excellent and lamentable Tragedie, of Romeo and *Iuliet*'. Elizabethan writers generally used the term 'Tragedy' loosely; it merely connoted a work in which events ended sadly rather than happily, and was not likely to have invoked elaborate definitions like Aristotle's in the *Poetics*. (In *Hamlet*, Polonius praises the actors for their versatility in offering 'scene individable or poem unlimited' – 'For the law of writ and the liberty, these are the only men' – suggesting that they can perform plays which respect principles of unity or which have free flexibility.[1])

The common abbreviation of the title, *Romeo and Juliet*, naturally calls to mind other Shakespearian tragedies of lovers: *Troilus and Cressida* and *Antony and Cleopatra*; and

25

to these should be linked *Othello*, since it deals so centrally
with the fatal relationship of the lovers Othello and Desdemona. If we consider this sequence in the most probable
chronological order – *Romeo and Juliet* (1595), *Troilus and
Cressida* (1602), *Othello* (1604) and *Antony and Cleopatra*
(1607) – a very significant pattern emerges. In each case there
is a background of strife which crucially affects the fortunes
of the lovers; the hero's involvement in conflict threatens
the survival of the love-relationship; the amatory is set in
pointed contrast to the bellicose; and there develops an extensive questioning of gender stereotypes, particularly the
stereotype associating the virile with the martial.

In *Romeo and Juliet*, both lovers are young (Romeo
possibly eighteen or so, Juliet thirteen); in *Troilus and
Cressida*, the eponymous figures seem somewhat older:
perhaps twenty and eighteen respectively. In *Othello*,
Desdemona may be under twenty, but Othello is certainly
middle-aged, a veteran of many travels and combats; and, in
Antony and Cleopatra, both protagonists are middle-aged.
The deaths of Romeo and Juliet are a consequence mainly of
the feud between Montagues and Capulets; had the feud not
led to Tybalt's death at Romeo's hands, Romeo would not
have been exiled to Mantua, and several tragic miscalcula-
tions need not have occurred; indeed, if there had been no
feud, Juliet might advantageously have named Romeo when
declining Paris: after all, her father deems Romeo 'a portly
gentleman; . . . . . a virtuous and well-govern'd youth'. In
Troilus and Cressida, the background is no mere familial
feud 'bred of an airy word' but the ten-year war between
Greeks and Trojans (even though Shakespeare deliberately
divests it of epic grandeur). Cressida's father summons her
to join him among the Greeks, and the lovers are parted;
eventually, Cressida proves unfaithful to Troilus. The contrast between the two plays is so telling as to seem deliberate,
as if Shakespeare desired, on the second occasion, to treat
both the love-relationship and its environment in a contrast-
ingly sceptical, even cynical mode. Compared with the
innocent ardour of Romeo and Juliet, who become man and

wife, there is a tainted, *appetitive* quality in the extra-marital relationship of Troilus and Cressida; again and again, imagery of food is used to describe their sexual longings; and, eventually, Troilus describes Cressida's infidelity thus:

> The fragments, scraps, the bits and greasy relics
> Of her o'er-eaten faith, are bound to Diomed.[2]

Troilus and Cressida sometimes reads like *Romeo and Juliet* rewritten by a cynic. Juliet proves her fidelity by suicide; but Cressida, with a worldly-wise, weary resignation, acquiesces in infidelity. The deaths of Romeo and Juliet at least serve to end the feud in Verona; in *Troilus and Cressida*, the futile war between Greeks and Trojans continues, Cressida remaining alive, Troilus going out fighting; the protagonists are not even granted the dignity of a poignant death-scene. Instead of a closure which resolves the issues, Pandarus advances to the front of the stage to mock the audience and promise to bequeath it his diseases. In its very structure, the play enacts the disorder which Ulysses had prophesied for and within the fictional world:

> Take but degree away, untune that string,
> And hark what discord follows. Each thing meets
> In mere oppugnancy . . . . .
> Then everything includes itself in power,
> Power into will, will into appetite;
> And appetite, an universal wolf,
> So doubly seconded with will and power,
> Must make perforce an universal prey,
> And last eat up himself.[3]

Troilus and Cressida was long regarded as a strangely unsatisfactory, problematic text. What critics generally overlooked was the subtle thematic co-ordination provided by that key-term, 'appetite'. For Shakespeare, 'appetite' connoted (1) ambition, particularly a greed for power; (2) the alimentary appetite: greed for food and drink; and (3) the sexual appetite, particularly the desire for sensual and illicit sexual gratification. The term thus links the play's war-material (for it is Paris' abduction of Menelaus' wife which has precipitated the Graeco-Trojan war), the flawed love-relationship of Troilus and Cressida (which, on Troilus' part, is all too sensuously appetitive), the theme of false valuation (based on the senses, as oppposed to true valuation based on moral judgement), the images of disease and the exceptionally large number of images of food. The disease imagery, which often invokes the venereal contagions transmitted by illicit sexuality, is thematically appropriate to a world of diseased judgement. Mercutio's 'A plague o' both your houses!' re-echoes as Troilus'

> Fools on both sides. Helen must needs be fair
> When with your blood you daily paint her thus.[4]

The war has a 'putrefièd core' at its centre (since Helen is not worth the ten years of bloodshed), and the contamination infects Troilus and Cressida too.

That Shakespeare had *Romeo and Juliet* in mind, as a basis for comparison and contrast, seems evident in the *aubade* scenes. In Act 3 Scene 5 of *Romeo and Juliet* occurs the famous *aubade*, when Juliet tries to persuade Romeo that they have been awakened by the song of 'the nightingale and not the lark'; but eventually, of course, she urges him, for safety's sake, to go. The counterpart-scene in *Troilus and Cressida*, IV.ii, is similar in situation but quite different in tone; the reluctance to part is mingled with a worldly wisdom; lyrical phrasing is offset by more staccato, conversationally realistic utterances:

TROILUS
    Dear, trouble not yourself. The morn is cold. . . . .
CRESSIDA Good morrow, then.
TROILUS I prithee now, to bed.
CRESSIDA Are you aweary of me?

TROILUS
   O Cressida! but that the busy day,
   Waked by the lark, hath roused the ribald crows,
   And dreaming night will hide our joys no longer,
   I would not from thee.
CRESSIDA   Night hath been too brief.
TROILUS
   Beshrew the witch! With venomous wights she stays
   As hideously as hell, but flies the grasps of love
   With wings more momentary-swift than thought.
   You will catch cold and curse me.
CRESSIDA Prithee, tarry. You men will never tarry.
   O foolish Cressid! I might have still held off,
   And then you would have tarried.[5]

'You will catch cold and curse me': there is a note of mundane realism; and the note of unillusioned worldly experience is sounded at 'I might have still held off, / And then you would have tarried'. The lyrically ardent commitment of Romeo and Juliet has given way to the flawed, less mutual, more worldly-wise exchange between Troilus and Cressida.

In *Othello*, the political background is the war between Turks and Venetians; and it is this which interrupts the lovers' honeymoon and dictates that relative isolation on the garrison-island of Cyprus which facilitates Iago's schemes. The subtler disruptive strife is a partly overt, partly covert racial strife. The racial prejudice so powerfully directed against Othello in the play's opening scenes helps to explain that cultural insecurity within him which makes him a prey to Iago's lies. Desdemona proves her love for the Moor by marrying him in spite of the barrier of race; but this very fact can be used by Iago as proof that she is likely to be adulterous. If she has been so unnatural as to betray her kinsmen and race, Iago argues, then she will be consistent by betraying her husband in order to copulate with a white gentleman, Cassio. The play is a delight to semioticians (students of signifying-systems), for it delights in 'reversed signs', ironic signifiers. Othello, though black (a colour which, the play emphasises, could connote evil, damnation and barbaric lust), is initially established as nobly civilised, a man of dignity, decency and wise judgement. The Machiavellian Iago seems to bear a sign proclaiming him honest (for all regard him as the 'honest' Iago). In his methods Iago could, indeed, be regarded as a perverse semiotician: a master of what Michael Riffaterre has called the 'praxis of the trans-formation'.[6] Perceiving that the world does not conform to his cynical beliefs about human nature, Iago seeks to trans-form the world paradoxically so that it appears to confirm those beliefs. The noble, poised, magnanimous Othello is goaded by Iago's slanders to the point where he does indeed seem a brutal barbarian; the virtuous and loyal Desdemona is made to seem, in her husband's eyes, a whore; the gentle-manly Cassio is transformed for a while into a drunken sot; an embroidered handkerchief, token of love, is made to seem proof of adultery. To a semiotician like Riffaterre, the 'heuristic' reading is a superficial registration of meaning, but the 'hermeneutic' reading elicits the underlying (and contrasting) significance. Iago's method is to persuade his dupes that their appraisals of others have been merely heuristic and should become hermeneutic. Othello is vul-nerable to Iago's lies because he is culturally insecure: he has travelled far from his noble Moroccan upbringing but has never been fully accepted in European society. The mo-ments of his death offer a superbly semiotic revelation of the nature of that fatal insecurity:

> And say besides that in Aleppo once,
> Where a malignant and a turbaned Turk
> Beat a Venetian and traduced the state,
> I took by th' throat the circumcisèd dog
> And smote him thus.
>   *He stabs himself*[.][7]

That suicidal thrust is the final reversed sign in a tragedy of reversed signs. As Othello stabs the imagined infidel, the enemy of the Venetian state, he simultaneously stabs General

Othello, the Christian defender of the Venetian state: foe and defender of civilisation are superimposed on each other, perishing together. Finally, he lies beside Desdemona on a bed which is a bier: black and white reconciled in death; as once, in an earlier play, a Montague, lying beside a Capulet in a funebral monument, had symbolised the reconciliation of hereditary foes.

In *Antony and Cleopatra*, the rhetoric of the lovers seeks to match the scale of the enterprise in which they are involved: the fate of the Roman empire itself. Married to Octavia but infatuated and obsessed by his love for Cleopatra, Antony fights Octavius and is defeated precisely because he lets his own military judgement be overruled by Cleopatra's; yet, in defeat, both die defiant. The struggle of Antony and Cleopatra is not only with Caesar, and not only with and for each other; it is also a struggle to define a love in which sexual desire, jealousy, intimate affection, majestic camaraderie, swaggering egotism, bitter remorse, and sublimely transcendent yearnings and affirmations are all interwoven. Their language invades and assails the ineffable, even in the act of declaring 'There's beggary in the love that can be reckoned'. Repeatedly Shakespeare invokes moral judgements – often scathingly hostile moral judgements – of the two protagonists, but only, finally, to make more sharp the conflict between, on the one hand, customary ethical criteria and, on the other hand, the ontological criterion which, in defiance of the ethical, values sheer aspiring fullness of being and seeks expression in eruptive and world-ransacking hyperboles.

As we look back over this sequence of tragedies, we see that *Romeo and Juliet* marks the beginning of an ever-deepening, ever-widening exploration of the nature of love and its tragic potentialities. From that early emphasis on poignantly innocent yet ill-fated rapture, through the dramatisation of Troilus' disillusionment and Othello's jealousy, to the final self-willed, self-generated apotheoses of Antony and Cleopatra, an expanding gamut of emotional experience has been peerlessly displayed. In order to define and test the mutuality of love, Shakespeare's dialectical imagination deploys a changing context of lethal hatred and belligerence. The innocent intensity of Romeo and Juliet establishes a model by which the more complex yet corruptible relationships can be gauged. Furthermore, a familiar yet perilous stereotype of virile conduct is repeatedly dramatised and questioned. Is truly virile conduct brave, heroic, aggressive, martial? Is sexual love a fulfilment of virility or a feminising enfeeblement? At a crucial moment in *Romeo and Juliet* (iii.i.115), Romeo complains:

> O sweet Juliet,
> Thy beauty hath made me effeminate
> And in my temper soften'd valour's steel.

Marriage to Juliet has made him Tybalt's kinsman; yet friendship with Mercutio makes him Tybalt's foe. Opting for the aggressive stereotype of virile conduct, he kills Tybalt and precipitates disaster for Juliet and himself. In those subsequent plays, Troilus, Othello and Antony all experience the fear that their martial identity may be undermined and 'made effeminate' by the love-relationship; Antony offers Cleopatra the bitter reproach:

> You did know
> How much you were my conqueror, and that
> My sword, made weak by my affection, would
> Obey it on all cause.[8]

Judged by the criterion of poetic quality, the conception of martial virility often received as much imaginative assent from Shakespeare as did the contrasting conception of amatory virility; so it is not the least achievement of *Romeo and Juliet* that eventually the former is so clearly linked to futile destructiveness and the latter to civilised harmony. Like Shakespeare's great feminist play *Love's Labour's Lost* (which was probably written at the same period),

Romeo and Juliet often proves to be unusually incisive in its questioning of stereotypes.

THE PLOT

Conventional Plot-summary

In *The Oxford Companion to English Literature*, Margaret Drabble offers the following synopsis of *Romeo and Juliet*.

> The Montagues and Capulets, the two chief families of Verona, are bitter enemies. Escalus, the prince, threatens anyone who disturbs the peace with death. Romeo, son of old Lord Montague, is in love with Lord Capulet's niece Rosaline. But at a feast given by Capulet, which Romeo attends disguised by a mask, he sees and falls in love with Juliet, Capulet's daughter, and she with him. After the feast he overhears, under her window, Juliet's confession of her love for him, and wins her consent to a secret marriage. With the help of Friar Laurence, they are wedded next day. Mercutio, a friend of Romeo, meets Tybalt, of the Capulet family, who is infuriated by his discovery of Romeo's presence at the feast, and they quarrel. Romeo comes on the scene, and attempts to reason with Tybalt, but Tybalt and Mercutio fight, and Mercutio falls. Then Romeo draws and Tybalt is killed. The prince, Montague, and Capulet come up, and Romeo is sentenced to banishment. Early next day, after spending the night with Juliet, he leaves Verona for Mantua, counselled by the friar, who intends to reveal Romeo's marriage at an opportune moment. Capulet proposes to marry Juliet to Count Paris, and when she seeks excuses to avoid this, peremptorily insists. Juliet consults the friar, who bids her consent to the match, but on the night before the wedding drink a potion which will render her apparently lifeless for 42 hours. He will warn Romeo, who will rescue her from the vault on her awakening and

carry her to Mantua. The friar's message to Romeo miscarries, and Romeo hears that Juliet is dead. Buying poison, he comes to the vault to have a last sight of Juliet. He chances upon Count Paris outside the vault; they fight and Paris is killed. Then Romeo, after a last kiss on Juliet's lips, drinks the poison and dies. Juliet awakes, and finds Romeo dead by her side, and the cup still in his hand. Guessing what has happened, she stabs herself and dies. The story is unfolded by the friar and Count Paris's page, and Montague and Capulet, faced by the tragic results of their enmity, are reconciled.[9]

That is one possible summary of *Romeo and Juliet*. It seems accurate enough, with the exception of the claim that Romeo 'wins her consent'. When he says that he seeks her 'faithful vow', Juliet replies 'I gave thee mine before thou didst request it'; and it is she who specifies a speedy marriage-day:

If that thy bent of love be honourable,
Thy purpose marriage, send me word tomorrow. . . . .

Drabble's error is significant: a conventional sense of the male as the dominant wooer has imposed itself on the text's unconventional depiction of Juliet. Otherwise, the synopsis seems sound. For our purposes, its value lies as much in what it omits as in what it suggests.

The plot-summary may hold some limited value for a novice: it may help to guide him or her, at the first reading, through the unfolding narrative. It may also have some limited value for a person who has read the play already but needs a simple reminder of some of its features. Although virtually every critical discussion of the work (however sophisticated or selective) entails reference to its plot, a plot-summary alone is practically useless as an indicator of merit. Reduced to a brief synopsis, a tragedy becomes indistinguishable from a third-rate melodrama, and a vivid satire resembles an implausible farce. The summary inevitably omits or conceals the intensities, the ardours, the shifts in tone, mood and pace, the vitalities of the contrasting individuals, the diverse richnesses of linguistic embodiment. It gives disproportionate space to complicated manœuvres. The relationship between the synopsis, the full text and the play in performance is, perhaps, analogous to the relationship between a small drawing of a skeleton, a film of a living person, and a direct observation of that person. Juxtaposition of the three reveals some resemblances; but simultaneously it emphasises the huge disparities.

The summary at least indicates the economical clarity and firmness of the plotting. Compared with Shakespeare's previous tragedy, the grotesquely gory *Titus Andronicus*, and compared with some of the later tragedies (notably *King Lear*, with its very complex structure), there is a linear clarity to *Romeo and Juliet* provided by its concentration on the story of the meeting, fulfilment, separation and deaths of the lovers. Almost everything in the play seems to be functional and in sharp focus; it lacks the complications and erratic movements in plotting which we encounter in, say, *Hamlet*, *King Lear* or *Antony and Cleopatra*. One test of the functionality of *Romeo and Juliet* is to seek a scene or speech which initially appears digressive or redundant: it will usually be found to contribute valuably to the total structure. Take, for instance, Mercutio's famous 'Queen Mab' speech (i.iv.53–103). It's a celebrated 'aria' or spectacular rhetorical feat, inviting a display of expressive virtuosity by the actor; and it may at first seem to be fanciful material which Shakespeare happened to have by him – perhaps originally written with *A Midsummer Night's Dream* in mind, since the speech has resemblances to Puck's self-description there (ii.i.43–57). Look at the 'Queen Mab' speech again, however, and it proves to have multiple functions. First, it fully establishes the engaging character of Mercutio as one who revels in mockingly witty display: a characteristic which will eventually help to cause his dispatch by Tybalt. Next, the bawdy reference–

This is the hag, when maids lie on their backs,
That presses them and learns them first to bear,
Making them women of good carriage

–maintains a theme established in the previous scene, when
both the Nurse and Juliet's mother envisaged in different
ways the time when Juliet would lie on her back beneath a
lover. Thirdly, Mercutio's conclusion declares,

I talk of dreams,
Which are the children of an idle brain,
Begot of nothing but vain fantasy,

and this proves to be hugely ironic in a play whose action is
given metaphysical resonance by premonitory dreams. So
Mercutio's set piece, though initially seeming centrifugal,
proves centripetal; and its lyrical fantasy touches repeatedly
on hard realities; its web of verbal gossamer captures
everyday substantialities, so its very texture reflects one of
the major features of the play: the combination of aspiring
lyricism and realistic muscularity.

Certainly, an audience's sense of the work's economical
clarity may be craftily aided by the directorial habit of
cutting the text of stage or screen productions. In practice,
the play's sequences of protracted lamentation are often
shortened. These sequences include Juliet's and Romeo's
lamentations at the sentence of banishment (iii.ii.108–26,
iii.iii.12 ff.) and the rather stylised mourning at Juliet's
supposed death (iv.v.23–64). In the latter case, the rhetorical
grief of the Capulets, Paris and the Nurse verges on the
parodic and may even bring to mind the burlesque of
mourning in *A Midsummer Night's Dream*, Act 5 Scene 1.
Another speech that seems to invite pruning is the Friar's
long explanation of events to the Prince. 'I will be brief', he
says; but he then proceeds to furnish forty lines of detailed
recapitulation. What makes it tedious is that, though en-
lightening the Duke, it reports what we know well already;
what may justify it is that the events summarised are thereby

submitted for the Prince's formal judgement and moralistic interpretation: turbulent, emotional occurrences are subjected to a rational closure which simultaneously ratifies the Prince's political authority.

This final judgement is, of course, a public judgement. One feature of *Romeo and Juliet* which structurally is highly important is the interweaving of private and public life. The plot as it unfolds moves adroitly between the bustle of the streets, the activities of Capulet's household, and the private world of the lovers. There is a co-ordinated variety of contrast: public brawls and discords, private embraces and harmonies; ceremonial edicts, informal jesting; older folks' reminiscences, young lovers' anticipations; festivity and mourning; rapt stillness, rapid action; social comedy, lonely disaster; union in love, union in death. Hence the dramatic liveliness of the play as a whole: aesthetically the contrasts are mutually enriching, mutually defining. Furthermore, via Mercutio, Capulet and the Nurse, the ample comedy is strongly integrated with the emergent tragedy. Mercutio's irreverent gusto, his irrepressibly provocative mockery, leads to his death by Tybalt's hand. Consequently, although the suicides of Romeo and Juliet have many causes, it may be said that one paradoxical source of their tragedy is the exuberant spirit of comedy.

The Double Time-Scheme

In some of his plays, notably *The Comedy of Errors* and *The Tempest*, Shakespeare maintains a taut and consistent time-scheme; but more frequently the chronology in his plays is loose, flexible and even inconsistent. As early as 1693, Thomas Rymer, in his *Short View of Tragedy*, scornfully drew attention to what was subsequently termed the 'double time-scheme' of *Othello*.[10] Iago, tempting Othello into jealousy of Cassio, talks as though several weeks at least have elapsed since Desdemona's marriage; and, for Othello's jealousy to have plausibility, we too must imagine this to be the case. Yet (excluding the voyage from Venice to

Cyprus, which is irrelevant to Iago's scheme, as Cassio and Desdemona are in separate ships) the main action takes no more than three days, and therefore affords no opportunity for the *sustained* adultery that Iago alleges. After their marriage, Othello and Desdemona spend two nuptial nights together (though both are interrupted); on the third night, he kills her. Shakespeare has so forcefully compressed the diffuse time-span of the source-tale that a split develops between what may be termed the chronology of enactment and the chronology of motivation. (The argument that Desdemona might have copulated with Cassio *before* marriage is contradicted by the text's emphasis, particularly at III.ii.169–281, on Othello's supposed misfortune as a husband whose wife subsequently cuckolded him.)

Othello thus presents in extreme form an inconsistency between the temporal 'foreground' and 'background' that we find elsewhere. In both *Love's Labour's Lost* and *Measure for Measure*, for instance, the main events span a few days, but some subsidiary events inconsistently span weeks or months.[11] In *Romeo and Juliet*, the 'short' time-scheme is highly conspicuous and rapid: what in Brooke's *Romeus and Juliet* was diffuse and protracted has become taut and compressed. As we have noted, this gives the play as a whole an impetuous rapidity of momentum and greatly facilitates ironies. The main time-scheme is very clear. Act 1 Scene 1 begins around 8.55 a.m. on Sunday, for it has 'but new struck nine' when Benvolio encounters Romeo later in that scene. Capulet's ball, where Romeo meets Juliet, takes place that evening. The clandestine marriage of the lovers is solemnised on Monday; an hour later, Romeo kills Tybalt. Romeo and Juliet spend that night together and part at dawn, Romeo leaving for banishment in Mantua. On Tuesday, in a harsh irony, Capulet (delighted by Juliet's feigned acquiescence) brings forward from Thursday to Wednesday the time appointed for her wedding to Paris. On Tuesday night, Juliet takes the sleeping-potion; on Wednesday she is entombed; Romeo hastens to her and to his death; and the final scene, with its discoveries and reconciliation, ends around dawn on Thursday. Thus, the main action appears to elapse within four days – indeed, within ninety-four hours.

The contrasting sense of a longer time-scheme is evoked by various references. In Act 2 Scene 4, the Nurse, speaking of Juliet, tells Romeo: 'I anger her sometimes and tell her that Paris is the properer man' (i.e. that Paris is a worthier suitor than Romeo). This gives the impression that Romeo has been a suitor for a considerable time, possibly weeks, even though he had met Juliet only thirteen hours or so previously. In Act 3 Scene 5, Lady Capulet proposes to send a poisoner to kill Romeo at Mantua, 'Where that same banish'd runagate doth live'; and Juliet laments that the Nurse, who now disparages Romeo, 'hath prais'd him . . . . . above compare / So many thousand times', which again invokes a time-scale of weeks at least. In the next scene, the Friar, with strange specificity (strange, for it seems to introduce an easily avoidable inconsistency), states that the potion's soporific power lasts for precisely 'two and forty hours'. This detail, coupled with our sense that Mantua, as a place of exile, must be a significant riding-distance from Verona (the actual distance being over twenty miles), lends further ambiguity to the time-scheme; and the Friar's specification is supported by the Watchman's subsequent claim at the vault that Juliet (discovered 'newly dead' after her suicide) 'here hath lain this two days burièd'. In short, whereas the dominant time-scheme compresses the action into four days, the subordinate time-scheme implies a period between five days and several weeks or more.

One explanation is that Shakespeare often was mathematically impatient and inconsistent: this view is supported by the inconsistent references to the passage of time in *The Winter's Tale*, by Claudius' impossible wager in *Hamlet*, by the famous oddity that Hamlet is a thirty-year-old student, and by Lady Capulet's varying age. (At i.iii.71–3 she seems to be relatively young, possibly as young as 28; but at v.iii.206 she refers to her 'old age'.) The problem can be relegated as a pseudo-problem by claiming that audiences in

the theatre are so credulously receptive to what is immediately presented, scene by scene, that they (unlike scholars
in their studies, who can turn back the pages to assess con-
sistency) are unlikely to notice such anomalies. A more
diligent response may be as follows. The explicit and sys-
tematic nature of the main, short time-scheme shows that
Shakespeare deliberately compressed Brooke's time-scale in
order to increase dramatic momentum, suspense and irony.
The 'long time' references by Juliet and the Nurse show that
for local emotional and psychological effect, he occasionally
neglected (perhaps deliberately, probably inadvertently) the
former scheme. The Friar's anomalous specificity implies an
author who has not yet worked out in detail the chronology
of subsequent events, and the Watchman's reference was
probably prompted by a memory of the Friar's specification. The extant authorial revisions to the text do not include
any changes to reduce the number of chronological anomalies, which suggests that Shakespeare, if aware of them, was
untroubled by them. This should not, however, oblige us to
make deferential defences of the kind offered by Granville-
Barker, who declared: 'There is, indeed, less of carelessness
than a sort of instinctive artistry about it.'[12] The fact is that
the anomalous 'long time' references could easily have been
corrected, and the play would have been even better as a
result: critics would then have been able to rejoice at Shakespeare's mastery of a taxingly taut chronology, just as they do
when praising the remarkable chronological elegance of *The
Tempest*.

FLUKE OR FATE? THE STRUCTURAL
PARADOX

One strong criticism of *Romeo and Juliet*, as the 'Critical
History' section showed, is that the tragic crisis lacks
'inevitability': the deaths of Romeo and Juliet stem from
rank bad luck, and thus lack the profound fatality which has
been deemed an essential of great tragedies.

It is obviously true that the plot depends on seemingly random occurrences. For example: in Act 1, Capulet entrusts the party invitations to a messenger who is unable to read; the messenger therefore consults a passer-by, who just happens to be Romeo; Romeo thus learns of the festivities, and decides to attend them in order to see Rosaline; and thus he chances to encounter Juliet. In Act 3, Romeo seeks to part the combatants in the street-fight, and the unintended result is that Mercutio, impeded by Romeo's arm, is mortally stabbed by Tybalt. Above all, there is the absurd delay of Friar Laurence's letter to Romeo: 'absurd' not only because the somewhat farcical obtrudes itself at a crucial point but also because the playwright's arrangement of events here seems uncharacteristically maladroit. Laurence entrusts his letter to Friar John (a new character introduced inelegantly late in the play), and hapless John is trapped for a while in a house at Padua because there has been an outbreak of plague – an outbreak of which there has been no mention previously. The chance event seems rather clumsily contrived. Again, if Friar Laurence had arrived only a few minutes earlier at the monument, if Romeo had arrived only a few minutes later, and if Juliet had awakened only a minute sooner, the disaster might have been averted. Hence the painful quality of the plotting in Act 5: we think, 'If only, if only . . . So near and yet so far'.

There are two preliminary points to be made. The first, as we have previously noted, is that the critical demand for 'inevitability' already has a somewhat dated air, since Brechtian principles and kindred modern literary theories have suggested that any literary work which depicts suffering as metaphysically-ordained may thereby inculcate a fatalistic and politically conservative attitude. A related – and questionable – assumption is that readers who have a religious disposition (or at least a nostalgia for religious values) will be inclined to value a literary work which implies divine providence; while readers who have a sceptical, secular disposition will prefer works which imply that the heavens are empty, and for them the agency of chance may seem more plausible than the hand of the gods or of God. Political correlations with these views are variable, but socialistic critics tend to assume (often rashly) that the 'providentialists' will be relatively conservative and the sceptics relatively left-wing. In *Radical Tragedy*, Jonathan Dollimore declares: 'Providentialism . . . . . constituted an ideological underpinning for ideas of absolute monarchy and divine right'; and so, for him, the 'progressive' texts of Shakespeare's era are those like *The Revenger's Tragedy*, in which 'providentialism is obliquely but conclusively discredited'.[13]

The second preliminary point is that even the major, 'mature' tragedies of Shakespeare, with which *Romeo and Juliet* has often been demeaningly compared, are not free from crucial coincidences. In *Othello*, Desdemona just happens to drop a handkerchief which later can be cited by Iago as crucial evidence of her adultery with Cassio; furthermore, Bianca unpredictably returns it to Cassio in the very minutes when Othello is eavesdropping on the conversation of Cassio and Iago. In *King Lear*, the infidelity of Goneril is revealed to Albany because Edgar, by slaying Oswald, has fortuitously intercepted her letter to Edmund; and, later, the delay which prevents the saving of Cordelia's life is presented as dependent on absent-mindedness by Albany: 'Great thing of us forgot!', he exclaims. Nevertheless, when all such allowances have been made, it is still clear that *Romeo and Juliet* depends in its plotting on more (and more conspicuous) coincidences than we customarily find in Shakespearian tragedy. A striking structural paradox then emerges.

On the one hand, the plot-structure seems full of flukes, of apparently fortuitous occurrences. On the other hand, in contrast, we encounter the following features:

1. Interpretative 'framing' devices: prominent proleptic and analeptic speeches (one at the outset, several at the denouement) which suggest that the main sequence of events is divinely ordained.

2. Numerous speeches of foreboding, which, being vindicated by the outcome, imply that certain characters are repeatedly attuned to some supernatural ordinance.
3. A strongly ironic patterning of events. If we see a pattern, we may infer a pattern-maker; so, again, a metaphysical design may be indicated.

Let us consider these in turn.

The 'Framing' Devices

At the outset, the Prologue stresses that Romeo and Juliet have a metaphysically-ordained role: they are to be the scapegoats or sacrifices necessary for the termination of their parents' feud:

> From forth the fatal loins of these two foes
> A pair of star-cross'd lovers take their life,
> Whose misadventur'd piteous overthrows
> Doth with their death bury their parents' strife.

Furthermore, only such sacrifices could suffice for the purpose: the Prologue says that otherwise 'nought could remove' the 'continuance of their parents' rage'. This speech has a potent proleptic effect, schooling our responses to subsequent events and giving strong resonance to the various moments of premonition which follow. Eventually, in Act 5 Scene 3, Laurence and the Duke echo the Prologue's theme. When Laurence finds Romeo dead, he tells Juliet:

> A greater power than we can contradict
> Hath thwarted our intents[;]

and later, when he explains matters to the Duke, he refers to the tragedy as 'this work of heaven'. The Duke, in turn, clearly interprets the sequence of events as God's plan to end the feud:

Where be these enemies? Capulet, Montague,
See what a scourge is laid upon your hate,
That heaven finds means to kill your joys with love;
And I, for winking at your discords too,
Have lost a brace of kinsmen. All are punish'd.

Certainly, the critic H. B. Charlton has argued that there is
a contradiction between the play's claim that only the
sacrifice of the lovers could suffice to end the feud and, in
contrast, the evidence that the feud is already moribund.[14]
Capulet reflects in Act 1 Scene 2, that ''tis not hard. . . . . /
For men so old as we to keep the peace', and later, at the ball,
he vigorously if temporarily restrains Tybalt's wrath.
Charlton makes insufficient allowance, however, for the
fact that the unreflective bellicosity of the servants, the
recalcitrant vengefulness of Tybalt, and even Paris's hostility to the 'vile Montague', all show that the fires of the feud
can still flare up readily and lethally.

Speeches of Foreboding and Related Intuitions

As early as Act 1 Scene 4, Romeo, on his way to the
Capulets' ball, says:

. . . . . my mind misgives
Some consequence yet hanging in the stars
Shall bitterly begin his fearful date
With this night's revels, and expire the term
Of a despisèd life clos'd in my breast
By some vile forfeit of untimely death.
But he that hath the steerage of my course
Direct my suit.

His intuition echoes the Chorus's reference to the fateful
stars; and, when he expresses his submission to God's will,
he does so in terms which introduce a recurrent image of
himself as a piloted vessel – a vessel eventually (v.iii.116–18)
to be shipwrecked. At i.v.117–19, Romeo, on learning that

Juliet is of the Capulet family, declares: 'O dear account. My life is my foe's debt'; and he sees an ominous significance (unintended by Benvolio) in Benvolio's 'Away, be gone, the sport is at the best' – that is, 'We should leave before events turn from good to bad'. Romeo's premonition is soon echoed by Juliet, who, in Act 2 Scene 2, fears that their match is 'too rash, too unadvis'd, too sudden, / Too like the lightning'. The imagery of sudden consuming fire is sustained in II.vi.1–15, a sequence in which Romeo declares that when the marriage has taken place, 'Then love-devouring death do what he dare', and Friar Laurence responds:

> These violent delights have violent ends
> And in their triumph die, like fire and powder,
> Which as they kiss consume.

When Romeo descends from Juliet's balcony after their night together, she says (III.v.54–6):

> O God, I have an ill-divining soul!
> Methinks I see thee, now thou art so low,
> As one dead in the bottom of a tomb.

Her intuition is echoed in Romeo's 'I dreamt my lady came and found me dead' (v.i.6), even though here, with Sophoclean irony, he derives false hope from the dream.

By anticipating the sombre outcome of events, these premonitions strongly counteract the sense of 'mere chance, sheer bad luck'; and they are reinforced by a variety of references (notably III.ii.136–7, III.v.140, IV.v.35–40) associating Juliet with a marriage to Death. Capulet, deceived by Juliet's drugged state, makes a declaration which is false at the time but unwittingly prophetic:

> There she lies,
> Flower as she was, deflowered by him.
> Death is my son-in-law, Death is my heir.
> My daughter he hath wedded.

Ironic Patterning

Romeo and Juliet is packed with ironies ranging from obvious, large-scale structural ironies to minute verbal ironies. In such cases, irony becomes evident to us either when we, from a position of superior knowledge, observe misunderstandings resulting from inadequate knowledge, or when we perceive some unintended or covert connection between different events or statements. Sometimes the connection may become overt when it is also perceived by a character (or characters); but even then, the character's perception may be tardier than ours.

First: perhaps the most prominent of the play's ironies is that the feud, which is a major cause of the deaths of the lovers, is ended by those deaths: their tragic self-sacrifices for love have a beneficent outcome which they did not foresee or intend. A related irony is that Friar Laurence had facilitated the lovers' clandestine marriage in the hope that it would bring about an end to the feud; and so it does, though not in the way he had intended. The inception of Romeo's love for Juliet has multiple ironies. He gatecrashes Capulet's feast in the hope of seeing Rosaline, whom he has declared peerless and for whom he has professed unalterable love; but his allegiance changes as soon as he sets eyes on Juliet. Benvolio had told him previously to reappraise his love by comparing Rosaline with others at the feast; and Romeo had hubristically declared that the comparison would only confirm her superiority. A related irony is that Capulet had given similar advice to Paris: remarking that Juliet was vulnerably young to be considered for marriage, Capulet had asked Paris to attend the feast and compare Juliet with the other women present. The comparison which changes Romeo's desires only confirms Paris's; had these consequences been reversed, there would have been no tragedy. When Mercutio, in II.i.17–29, conjures Romeo by rehearsing Rosaline's charms, the irony bounces in both directions: against Mercutio, who is unaware of Romeo's change of heart, and against Romeo, whose impetuous amatory *volte-face* is thus emphasised. The comic potential of the lover's transferred allegiance is exploited again, not only when the Friar (at II.iii.40) exclaims 'God pardon sin. Wast thou with Rosaline?' – one of the most tellingly comic lines in the play – but also when Mercutio (II.iv.13–14) declares that Romeo is mortally stricken by *Rosaline's* beauty.

Romeo's uninvited attendance at the feast, which brings him the brief joy of his love for Juliet, serves to antagonise Tybalt, who therefore seeks a duel with Romeo, and thereby courts his own death. In Act 3 Scene 1, Tybalt and Mercutio are puzzled by Romeo's initial reluctance to enter the duel; neither of them knows, as we do, that since Romeo is newly married to Juliet, Tybalt has become a relative – a kinsman – of Romeo. Seeking to halt the strife, Romeo intervenes in the sword-fight between Tybalt and Mercutio; the ironic unintended consequence is that Tybalt mortally wounds Mercutio, and Romeo is then led to avenge his friend in a combat which results in the kinsman's death and in Romeo's banishment. The well-meant intervention has several fatal consequences. The banishment, in turn, causes the death from grief of Romeo's mother (reported in v.iii.209–10).

A further cluster of ironies emerges in the events following the banishment. Being clandestinely married to Romeo, Juliet defies her father's wish that she should marry Paris, which makes Capulet the more insistent. On the Friar's advice, Juliet agrees to the match; but her delighted father then, unexpectedly, brings forward by one day the intended time of the nuptial. Capulet also says that the change results from his desire to end as soon as possible Juliet's apparent grief at Tybalt's death, Capulet being unaware that Juliet is really grieving at Romeo's banishment. Juliet's defensive deceit thus serves to ensnare her. The day of the intended marriage becomes, in a reversal bitterly registered by Capulet and Paris, the day of funeral. One of the most blatantly ironic scenes in the play is that (IV.v.14–95) in which the Nurse, Capulet, his wife and Paris all lament the 'death' of Juliet, who is thought to have been overcome by sorrow for

Tybalt. Of crueller blatancy is the culminating sequence in which Romeo kills himself, mistakenly believing – like the Capulets and Paris – that Juliet is dead; if a little more time had first elapsed, he might have been joyfully reunited with her; instead, as a consequence of his suicide, Juliet herself perishes.

The plot establishes a running irony of *impeded messages* – messages variously misdirected or retarded. In Act 1 Scene 2, Capulet entrusts the invitation-list to a servant who cannot read; the servant asks Romeo to decipher it; as a kindly afterthought, Romeo does so, and thus learns of the feast. His presence there enrages Tybalt. According to Benvolio (in Act 2 Scene 4), the infuriated Tybalt consequently sends Romeo a letter challenging him to a duel. The letter is not received by Romeo, for he has been away from home for the purpose of marrying Juliet, Tybalt's kinswoman. In Act 2 Scene 5, Juliet waits impatiently for the Nurse to return with a message from Romeo. The Nurse has already taken more than three hours on this local errand; and, when she returns, she teases Juliet by a tantalisingly digressive and tardy presentation of Romeo's instructions. Impeded communication evidently delights the Nurse, for, in Act 3 Scene 2, when bringing the news of Romeo's banishment, she torments Juliet by letting her believe for a considerable while that it is Romeo and not Tybalt who has been slain. The final instance in this sequence is the most famous or notorious (though now, in the light of these precedents, it may seem less arbitrary): Friar Laurence's crucial letter to Romeo is delayed and brought back to the Friar; whereas nothing delays Balthasar's arrival with the erroneous news that Juliet is dead. Consequently, Romeo's arrival at the tomb coincides with Paris's; each impedes the other; Paris's pious intention as a mourner leads to his death at Romeo's hand; the amatory rivals are united, and both share the tomb with Juliet and Tybalt. The final resolution of the feud has its ironic portent when Romeo, a Montague, falls dead within the traditional vault of the Capulets.

In short, *Romeo and Juliet* is particularly full of stark and interrelated ironies. No tragedy lacks ironies; but in this case they seem more sharp, keen and prominent than in many other tragedies. *Julius Caesar*, too, contains its fatal misunderstandings (notably Cassius' erroneous belief that Brutus has been slain, which leads him to choose death) as well as the familiar large-scale tragic pattern in which events have consequences drastically different from those intended; but *Julius Caesar* does not have that particularly poignant, 'so near and yet so far' quality of the dominant ironies in the earlier play. Antony and Cleopatra are doomed lovers, but their suffering never has that keenly touching poignancy of Romeo's and Juliet's. These differences can readily be understood. The protagonists of *Romeo and Juliet* are characterised by their innocent, ardent youth; in their progress there often seems to be merely a hair's breadth between disaster and potential happiness; the impetuous innocent commitment of the lovers proves fatal, but Laurence's fertile ingenuity *almost* succeeds. Above all, Romeo and Juliet move in a world in which authority (represented by the Duke) seems benignly reasonable, while the citizens, though sometimes rashly violent, have nothing of the evil that is so conspicuous in *Macbeth* or *King Lear*.

The three items we have been considering (the framing devices, the speeches of foreboding and the numerous ironies) illustrate various modes of patterning within *Romeo and Juliet*. Does the presence of patterning within a literary work imply that the fictional world is governed by a supernatural pattern-maker, some divine providential force? The answer is, 'Not necessarily.' The implications of ironic sequences within a text may be providential or anti-providential; we may infer benign, malign or absent supernatural agency. In *King Lear*, Albany says of Cordelia, 'The gods defend her!'; a second or so later Lear enters, with Cordelia dead in his arms. The effect is of a ruthless rebuttal of his pious plea. In Thomas Hardy's *Tess of the d'Urbervilles*, the cruel ironies veer between the implication that the heavens are empty and the implication that any presiding deity must be cruel: '[T]he

President of the Immortals, in Æschylean phrase, had ended his sport with Tess.'[15] In Samuel Beckett's *Waiting for Godot*, the ironies are similarly ambiguous; now atheistic (when they imply that there is no God and no Godot) and now antitheistic (when they imply that there is a malign deity who tantalises the tramps by repeatedly sending a boy to promise that Godot will soon arrive).

In *Romeo and Juliet*, the combination of the ironies, the forebodings and the framing devices certainly suggests a supernatural force which, while mocking various local hopes and aspirations, achieves an eventual good end (the reconciliation) by sacrificial means; so there is considerable support for the notion that the basic theology of the action is Christian, given not only Christianity's emphasis on sacrifice as the price of atonement but also the Friar's and the Prince's explicit interpretation of the events as 'this work of heaven'. There was also a doctrine, familiar to Shakespeare, which proffers a theological resolution of the main structural paradox that we have been considering. That doctrine, which harmonises the appearance of chance with a belief in providential ordinance, advocated the conception of *Fortune as God's agent*.

THE PARADOX OF FORTUNE

The ancient Roman goddess Fortuna was originally regarded as a bringer of fertility, but gradually she became identified with the Greek deity Tyche, the personification of chance. Probably in those times the relatively credulous would be confident of the deity's supernatural and objective status; the relatively sophisticated would regard her as a poetical fiction, 'a way of talking about' chance and change; and many people would hold an intermediate view, varying between the credulous and the sceptical.

In the medieval period, Christian writers sought to reconcile classical pagan entities with the dominant Christian theology. Particularly influential then was Boethius' *De*

Consolatione Philosophiæ (*Concerning the Consolation Afforded by Philosophy*). Written in Rome in the sixth century and partly indebted to Seneca, this Latin treatise was translated in the fourteenth century by Chaucer and, two centuries later, by Queen Elizabeth I. In the Chaucerian version, the Senecan doctrine was as follows. Fortune is a deity subordinate to God and forming part of his scheme for the universe. As she turns her wheel, so unfortunate mortals become fortunate, and vice versa. She ensures that worldly matters are subject to inconstancy; chance and insecurity become endemic. The wise man, however, perceives the way to reduce her power over him. Since she governs worldly matters, the wise man chooses to set his sights on heaven: he aspires to eternal felicity instead of sublunary fulfilments; and his Christian stoicism is rewarded with eventual eternal salvation. Thus, Fortune can be seen as a benevolent mentor to the perceptive individual; she teaches him to place little value on mortal gratifications. Hence the paradox that earthly disorder is evidence of eternal order.[16]

The modern reader may deem this doctrine a rather naïve attempt to fuse the pagan with the Christian, particularly as Fortune has no biblical warrant; but it displays some ingenuity as a way of dealing with one obvious objection to Christian belief. This objection is that though God is supposed to be a benevolent and omnipotent deity, the evidence of the senses tells us that life on earth is often chaotic and unjust. The Boethian scheme squares the circle, reconciling the fortuitous with the providential by postulating a world in which the appearance of the fortuitous has been designed by God as a way of testing faith and guiding the reflective individual towards a truly spiritual outlook. (Thus an ostensibly fatalistic notion is reconciled with free will and independent action, albeit of an ascetic, contemplative kind.) The more worldly a person is, the more that person will seem enslaved to chance; the less worldly, the more free from chance's inflictions. Alexander Pope, in the eighteenth century, would eventually epitomise the notion thus:

> All Nature is but Art, unknown to thee;
> All Chance, Direction, which thou canst not see;
> All Discord, Harmony, not understood;
> All partial Evil, Universal Good. . . . .[17]

Boethius' doctrine, loosely and variously apprehended, was widely pervasive in Elizabethan times: in literature of the period there are innumerable references to Fortune and her wheel and to the belief that while her boons may be deceptive, the vicissitudes she sends may teach valuable lessons in stoicism. In *King John* (iii.iv.119–20), Pandolf remarks:

> [W]hen Fortune means to men most good,
> She looks upon them with a threat'ning eye.

Hamlet praises Horatio (iii.ii.65–6) for being

> A man that Fortune's buffets and rewards
> Hath ta'en with equal thanks. . . . .

And Friar Laurence is a sound Boethian when he promises Romeo 'Adversity's sweet milk, philosophy'. Lovers were particularly vulnerable: in Kyd's *Soliman and Perseda*, Fortune declares: 'Why, what is *Loue* but *Fortunes* tenisball?'[18]

As we have seen, Brooke's *Romeus and Juliet* repeatedly invokes Fortune, aided by the stars, as the deity presiding over the action. Although Shakespeare's metaphysic is more fluid than Brooke's, the references in the play to Fortune and the stars (as at Romeo's famous cry, 'Then I defy you, stars!') are often resonant. When Romeo realises the implications of his slaying of Tybalt, he cries, 'O, I am fortune's fool!'; and, when he parts from Juliet to begin his exile, Juliet says:

> O Fortune, Fortune! All men call thee fickle;
> If thou art fickle, what dost thou with him

That is renown'd for faith? Be fickle, Fortune,
For then I hope thou wilt not keep him long,
But send him back.

(Fortune does indeed send him back – but to his death.)
When Laurence learns that the letter has miscarried, 'Unhappy fortune!' is his comment. Of course, the text's inconsistency in capitalisation (now 'Fortune', now 'fortune')
usefully indicates the ambiguity of the concept. The capital-
ised version tends to invoke the notion of an objective deity
with supernatural power over mortals; whereas 'fortune' is
more likely to suggest merely 'chance'.

The medieval assimilation of Fortune to Christianity was
nowhere more marked than in the early conception of
tragedy. As *De Consolatione Philosophiæ* had observed,
'What other thyng bywayles the cryinges of tragedyes but
oonly the dedes of Fortune. . . . . ?'[19] In *The Canterbury
Tales*, Chaucer's Monk defines tragedy as a story of one
who falls from prosperity to misery; and the Monk's tale,
listing examples of tragic figures, explains the Boethian
implications of the sequence.

For certein, when that Fortune list to flee,
Ther may no man the cours of hir withholde.
Lat no man truste on blynde prosperitee;
Be war by thise ensamples trewe and olde.[20]

This simplistic conception contrasts with the humanistic
conception which later emerged. In the Romantic and post-
Romantic period, the term 'tragedy' acquired a semi-
mystical aura: as A. C. Bradley remarked in 1904, 'tragedy
would not be tragedy if it were not a painful mystery'.[21] In
drama of the Elizabethan period, we see this modern conception, which stresses ambiguity and mystery, emerging
from the simplistic pattern of an exemplary rise and
downfall.

For poets and dramatists, one highly convenient feature
of the doctrine of Fortune was that it could serve as a

philosophical lubricant or rationale for the more erratic and
accident-bound narratives. A plot seemingly dependent on
fluke could thereby be invested with a certain measure of
philosophical dignity or respectability. An aura of metaphysical significance could be given to life's customary ups
and downs. We sometimes overlook the fact that the philosophical view offered by a Shakespeare play may be locally
opportunistic, in the sense that it may have been deployed as
a way of lubricating the available plot-mechanism; a different plot might invite a very different philosophical rationale.
A belief in the influence of the stars, endorsed in the
Prologue of *Romeo and Juliet*, is scornfully dismissed by
Cassius in *Julius Caesar* and Edmund in *King Lear* (though,
given that Cassius and Edmund are destructive conspir-
ators, Shakespeare may have deemed pietistic deference
preferable to sceptical egotism).[22] *Macbeth* strongly invokes
the conception of supernatural evil combated by Christian
virtue; but *Antony and Cleopatra* is predominantly secular,
though with glimpses of classical theology: the metaphysic
of each play is influenced by the dramatist's notion of its
historical period. In *Romeo and Juliet*, Shakespeare, prompted by Brooke, appears to have found the Boethian paradox
convenient as a co-ordinator of a plot which, while stressing
rapid and seemingly fortuitous reversals, yet implies a pro-
videntialist pattern of reconciliation.

Since Shakespeare's imagination is so strongly dialectical,
however, a contrasting 'humanist' metaphysic is also powerfully voiced. In this contrasting metaphysic, the ardour of
Romeo and Juliet is dramatised not as a perilous immersion
in the worldly which subjects them to the sway of Fortune
but as a quest for transcendence of the mundane by means of
a love-relationship so intense as to approach apotheosis; an
intensity which is its own validation and makes the pruden-
tialist considerations of Boethian asceticism seem a denial of
the glories attainable by ardent lovers. The authority of the
Friar's interpretation of disaster as 'the hand of heaven'
is weakened by his shameless theological charade when
interpreting Juliet's supposed death as her divine reward

(IV.v.65–83) *and* as divine punishment for sin (IV.v.94–5), while his advocacy of stoical courage seems belied by his eagerness to escape when the watchmen approach the tomb. Furthermore, if, in *Romeo and Juliet*, the closure of the action seems to voice a mystification or obfuscation of suffering (by depicting it as a divinely-ordained means of reconciliation), this may have provoked Shakespeare's dialectical imagination to offer, a few years later, the astonishingly disruptive, demystifying, 'open' ending of *Troilus and Cressida*.

THEMES AND IMAGERY

Scansion of the themes of a literary work tends to increase one's sense of the work's unity; indeed, such scansion may inevitably exaggerate a work's co-ordination. This is because themes tend to be rather capacious and elastic in nature; suspiciously, there are few narratives in which such themes as 'reality versus illusion', 'the test of time' or 'innocence versus experience' cannot be discerned. Nevertheless, thematic scansion can often reveal principles of organisation which are more supple and subtle than those required by the mechanics of plotting, and whose rendering may indeed have been motives of the author's creative imagination.

In a selective discussion, a good starting-place is Friar Laurence's ruminative speech at the opening of Act 2 Scene 3, since his soliloquy is itself, in part, a meditation on the thematic and metaphoric interpretation of particulars; certainly it demonstrates thematic elasticity. The Friar, gathering weeds and flowers, reflects that the earth is both nature's tomb and womb; that the vilest products of earth yield some goodness, while the best products may be abused:

> Virtue itself turns vice being misapplied,
> And vice sometime's by action dignified.

Indeed, one and the same flower may yield both medicine and poison; similarly, within each person opposed principles contend: 'grace and rude will': heavenly virtue and fleshly desire. The Friar has thus demonstrated analogies between the dualities of earth, earth's produce, and human nature. What he says seems basically traditional, homiletic, and (if we are familiar with Christian doctrine) rather platitudinous; but the sense of platitude evaporates when we see how well his maxims harmonise with the details and larger movements of the play. His sense of natural ambivalence tallies largely with the dialectical treatment of sexual desire, for example. Typically, between Romeo's ardently lyrical addresses to Juliet in Act 1 Scene 5 and Act 2 Scene 2 intervenes the sequence in which Mercutio exclaims, 'O that she were / An open-arse and thou a poperin-pear!' Romeo's exalted imagery of desire is repeatedly contrasted with such reductively carnal imagery of sexuality, as when (at ii.i.23–6) Mercutio's irrepressibly bawdy mind fuses conjuration and copulation:

> 'Twould anger him
> To raise a spirit in his mistress' circle
> Of some strange nature, letting it there stand
> Till she had laid it and conjur'd it down. . . . .

The active penis is an insistent covert image of the innuendoes. Yet, whether reductive or enhancive, the play's sexual imagery is usually so full of vitality as to elude or exceed the bounds of Friar Laurence's doctrinal scheme.

The Friar, though often wise and well-meaning, is subject to some ironic criticism, and unwittingly illustrates the perilous dualities – the intertwinings of good and bad – that he has mentioned. He assists the clandestine marriage of Romeo and Juliet, for, though it involves duplicity, he hopes thereby that a good end (converting the feud to an alliance) will justify the dubious means; but this leads to the further duplicity of the feigned death of Juliet, which, in turn, in spite of his best endeavours, results in four real deaths: those of Paris, Romeo, Juliet and Lady Montague. Yet, by a further irony, these unforeseen fatalities achieve his original

goal of reconciling the opposed houses. The conflict between 'grace and rude will' is (according to Christian theology) endemic in human nature; but the play gives vivid
illustration to this theme by showing signally how the good
and bad are intermixed in individuals. Capulet can be both
benevolent and tyrannical; Romeo, who seeks to act as
peace-maker, is nevertheless goaded by circumstances to be
the slayer both of Tybalt and Paris; while Capulet and
Montague, though formerly eager to enter the fray, can
eventually commiserate fraternally with each other. The
Friar's specific reference to the duality of the herb which
yields both medicine and poison is an acute anticipation of
the role played subsequently by both the sleeping-draught
which he regards as beneficent and the poison which will
slay Romeo. It may be noted that the theology of the play
proves undoctrinally liberal: by their suicides, Romeo and
Juliet have, according to Catholic doctrine, committed
mortal sin, against which the Friar had warned Romeo
(III.iii.115–17); but this doctrinal tenet is waived, and final
emphasis is placed firmly on a relatively humanistic response
to the tragic loss (the lovers are 'Poor sacrifices of our
enmity') and on the lesson of reconciliation that such
suicidal death teaches:

> See what a scourge is laid upon your hate,
> That heaven finds means to kill your joys with love. . . . .

We may note the contrast offered by *Hamlet*, in which
Ophelia, whose death seems the mere misadventure of
a deranged victim, is denied burial in sanctified ground
because of the priestly suspicion that she may have committed suicide.

The Friar himself, who on stage is most aptly played as if
he were about sixty years old, forms part of the thematic
account of the contrasts between youth and age. On the side
of youth, for better and for worse, there are energy, vitality
and ardour; on the side of age, for better and for worse, are
experience, an abundance of recollection, and the kinds of

authority lent by the passage of time. There can be rashness,
folly and violence on both sides. Indeed, one of Shakespeare's
main thematic preoccupations in *Romeo and Juliet* is clearly
the contrasting modes of apprehension of time. Through the
reminiscences of the older generation, we are reminded of the
customary long time-scale of human life: the long journey
from birth to marriage and copulation and thence to old age
and death. The lovers, in their impetuous progress, live far
more briefly but more intensely, and a keynote in their
dialogue is their impatience, their eagerness to seize the
moment of joy before it fades. This thematic contrast in
temporality was clearly intended by Shakespeare in his
adaptation of Brooke's narrative, particularly in his intensification of the speed of the central events. And while the human
drama is played out, the chronological arrangement and the
imagery both invoke the greater cycle of natural time
governed by the sun and the seasons. Reminders of the annual
cycle of procreation, of budding flowers, birds nesting, the
April awakening, are so profuse in the first half of the play as
to offset ironically the early deaths to be portrayed subsequently. The rapid action is carefully related to the sequence
of day and night: initially, Romeo is described as walking,
lovelorn and alone, at dawn; his first meeting with Juliet ends
at dawn; his parting for exile is another dawn-scene; and the
play ends with a sombrely protracted dawning:

> A glooming peace this morning with it brings:
> The sun for sorrow will not show his head.

Related imagery of light amid darkness often conveys the
theme of the radiant brevity of young love. In *Shakespeare's
Imagery*, Caroline Spurgeon wrote:

> The dominating image is *light*, every form and manifesta-
> tion of it: the sun, moon, stars, fire, lightning, the flash of
> gunpowder, and the reflected light of beauty and of love;
> while by contrast we have night, darkness, clouds, rain,
> mist and smoke.[23]

Illustrations include some of the most celebrated lyrical speeches:

> O, she doth teach the torches to burn bright.
> It seems she hangs upon the cheek of night
> As a rich jewel in an Ethiop's ear . . . . .
> The brightness of her cheek would shame those stars
> As daylight doth a lamp. Her eyes in heaven
> Would through the airy region stream so bright
> That birds would sing and think it were not night . . . . .

Indeed, Spurgeon's list covers several pages. Much of this 'light' imagery is basically conventional, familiar stuff for sonneteers and romance-writers, and partly derivative (of course) from Brooke; but repeatedly in the play it gains new eloquence and immediacy; and, as Spurgeon pointed out, such recurrent visual allusions are not only a matter of simile and metaphor, since the drama quite overtly exploits contrasts between light and darkness: as when Juliet's torch-illuminated body forms a region of brightness within the dark vault overshadowed by ominous night. Some of the images suggest dangerous and sudden brightness: lightning, explosives; as in these examples:

> Too like the lightning, which doth cease to be
> Ere one can say 'It lightens'. . . . .
> These violent delights have violent ends,
> And in their triumph die, like fire and powder,
> Which as they kiss consume.

In the last nine words, claimed Spurgeon, the Friar 'sums up the whole movement of the play';[24] and, though her claim simplifies and melodramatises the varied pace and elegiac close of the drama, it does bring to mind the fatal celerity of the main action.

A millennia-old mythic resonance is lent to *Romeo and Juliet* by the leitmotif of Death as Juliet's bridegroom. The notion is explicit at iii.ii.136–7, when Juliet declares:

> I'll to my wedding bed,
> And death, not Romeo take my maidenhead.

Later, Lady Capulet scornfully says: 'I would the fool were married to her grave'; while Juliet, distraught at the prospect of a bigamous marriage to Paris, pleads:

> Delay this marriage for a month, a week,
> Or if you do not, make the bridal bed
> In that dim monument where Tybalt lies.

In Act 4 Scene 5, the grieving Capulet declares to Paris:

> O son, the night before thy wedding day
> Hath Death lain with thy wife. . . . .

Most memorably of all, there is the imagery of Romeo's sensuously eloquent address to Juliet in the tomb:

> Why art thou yet so fair? Shall I believe
> That unsubstantial Death is amorous,
> And that the lean abhorrèd monster keeps
> Thee here in dark to be his paramour?
> For fear of that I still will stay with thee,
> And never from this palace of dim night
> Depart again.

The idea that a beautiful young woman may become the prey of amorous Death is stock material for elegiac verse and for amatory poetry in the *carpe diem* tradition; but, in the play, it is given unique force by the graphic symbolism of those moments in the tomb when Juliet lies living but unconscious, with her two mortal wooers dead at her side as though they had been vanquished by jealous Death.

Romeo and Juliet is a culturally proleptic drama: it anticipates by some two hundred years several of the main preoccupations of the Romantic movement. The Gothic novel's charnel-house horrors; the lyrical poets' invocations of natural beauty; the attempt to forge a surrogate religion of intense sexual desire; even the ironic interplay of the exalted and the mundane which characterises the most intelligent long poem of the era (Byron's *Don Juan*): all these have ample precedent in Shakespeare's play. The horrors of claustral death and decay, vividly and even histrionically evoked (notably by Juliet, iv.i.80–8, iv.iii.30–57), gain accentuated force in a drama which, particularly in its first three acts, has so profusely bred images of the vitality common to young people and their wide natural environment. The older spectators clearly relish this vitality: thus Capulet (i.ii.24–30):

> At my poor house look to behold this night
> Earth-treading stars that make dark heaven light.
> Such comfort as do lusty young men feel
> When well-apparell'd April on the heel
> Of limping winter treads, even such delight
> Among fresh female buds shall you this night
> Inherit at my house.

Even Friar Laurence shares this aesthetic enjoyment of youthful beauty (ii.vi.16–20):

> Here comes the lady. O, so light a foot
> Will ne'er wear out the everlasting flint.
> A lover may bestride the gossamers
> That idles in the wanton summer air
> And yet not fall; so light is vanity.

(His 'so light is vanity' effects a neat rescue of morality from empathy.)

In different ways, several of the main characters manifest descriptive gusto: whether it is Lady Capulet carrying to exceptional lengths the analogy between Paris and a book, Mercutio fantasising about Queen Mab, Romeo apostrophising Juliet, or Capulet and Laurence in those two cited examples, a relish for sustained analogies and pursued metaphors is widespread. Sometimes this enjoyment of creative description is assimilated to the characterisation; sometimes the characterisation is subordinated to it. Either way, the creative energy implicit in the play's profusion of imagery is, of course, one of its strongest positive characteristics. All the diverse human experiences of the work are constantly being invested with an eloquence which, in its tireless voicing of comparisons, enriches their significance and repeatedly epitomises memorably the fleeting moods.

· 4 ·

Aspects of Characterisation

THE CAST-LIST

If we look at the characters' names in the list of *dramatis personæ*, we see what in Shakespeare's plays is familiar and yet, on reflection, odd. The setting of *Romeo and Juliet* is Verona; but most of the names look English. Certainly some (Escalus, Romeo, Mercutio, Benvolio) are Latinate or Italianate; but others (Peter, Sampson, Gregory, Potpan, Laurence, John, Simon Catling, Hugh Rebeck, James Soundpost) are English. To a literary scholar, this use of anglicised or English names in a play supposedly about foreign people will seem such a familiar Shakespearian device as scarcely to be remarkable; that is how Shakespeare and many other Elizabethan writers commonly did treat foreign names. Nevertheless, there is one significant consequence. In the play before us, we are often reminded (by the explicit references to Verona, Mantua and other locations) of the Italian setting; but the anglicised or directly English names, coupled with the familiar use of distinctively English idioms, do tend to make an imaginative bridge

between the ostensibly foreign and the familiar British
activities; the names act as an imaginative lubricant, so that
our imagination readily slides between the far-away and the
close-to-home. The action takes place during a hot Italian
summer, late June; yet sometimes the climate evoked is
more English than Italian: at the wedding-feast, for example, Capulet calls for more logs for the fire.

Shakespeare's procedure is geographically, culturally and
linguistically inconsistent; even so, as we adapt to the convention, it makes sufficient imaginative sense. In return for
our conceptual flexibility we are granted not only the
enjoyment of a story which, in a venerable romantic
tradition, concerns the high passions of noble people in a
distant land, but also the pleasures of intelligent mimesis of
the everyday matters of a familiar social environment. The
contrasts and interactions of the two may be mutually
enriching and mutually critical.

Again, as is frequently the case in Shakespearian cast-lists,
some of the names have symbolic resonance, some have historic associations, and many seem simply arbitrary. Several
illustrate Shakespeare's remarkable aptitude in exploiting
verbal connotations. 'Romeo' is Shakespeare's adaptation
of Brooke's 'Romeus', but Shakespeare has exploited (as
Brooke had not) the Italian resonance of the name. The
Italian noun *romeo* means 'pilgrim'; in 1598, John Florio's
dictionary translated it as 'palmer' (a pilgrim whose palm-
leaf shows that he has visited the Holy Land); and the
famous sonnet in which Romeo and Juliet have their first
exchange of dialogue develops elaborately the apt conceit
that Romeo is a pilgrim or palmer visiting a shrine or
beseeching a saint. 'Juliet' ('Giulietta' in Italian) is an appropriate name for a child born in July; Brooke made no explicit
connection with the month, but Shakespeare lets the Nurse's
free reminiscences establish specifically that Juliet was born
on 31 July. In *Romeus and Juliet*, Mercutio makes only a
very brief appearance; we are told that he has a high
reputation for courteous speech and pleasant ways; that
when among 'bashfull maydes' he is bold as a lion; and that

he has peculiarly cold hands. Shakespeare, once again, has exploited the connotations of the name: 'Mercutio' connoted 'mercurial' (quick-witted, lively and loquacious, Mercury being the Roman god of eloquence, *mercurio* being Italian for quicksilver), and Mercutio thus becomes one of the most memorably witty and lively characters in Shakespearian drama. 'Benvolio' means 'well-wishing, benevolent', and, by repeatedly trying to act as a peace-maker, Benvolio (who had not figured in Brooke's poem) shows that his character is consonant with his name. The 'Tibalt' of *Romeus and Juliet* ('Teobaldo' anglicised) was as fiercely aggressive as is his counterpart in the play; but a new development is that Shakespeare has exploited the feline associations of the name. 'Tybalt' was traditionally a cat's name; even today, the variant 'Tibbles' is commonly given to feline pets; Shakespeare's contemporary, Thomas Nashe, refers to 'Tibault . . . . . Prince of Cattes'; and hence Mercutio refers to Tybalt as 'More than Prince of Cats', 'Good King of Cats' and 'a cat, to scratch a man to death'. His character is evidently cat-like in its lithe energy, predatory vigilance and relish for territorial combat.

Other names are less resonant. 'County Paris' derives directly from Brooke, 'County' being an anglicisation of the Italian *conte* (count or earl). 'Escalus' derives from 'della Scala', Bartolommeo della Scala being a famous ruler of Verona in the early fourteenth century, the period in which da Porto and Bandello set the tale of Romeo and Juliet. 'Montagues' and 'Capulets' are anglicisations of 'Montecchi' and 'Capelletti'. 'Angelica' proves to be an ironic misnomer for the worldly and (at times) cynical nurse. Other surnames are derived from the characters' occupations: for example, Grindstone (i.v.9), Potpan, Rebeck (a rebeck being a kind of viol), Soundpost (a soundpost being part of a violin) and Catling (i.e. 'Lute-string').

These nomenclatural conventions correspond broadly to the linguistic conventions of the play (whereby nobler characters are more likely to speak in poetry, the lower characters more likely to speak in prose), and we may notice

that the political hierachy within the fictional world is thus
subtly – sometimes subliminally – reinforced.

CHARACTERISATION AND THE
CONVENTIONS OF DISCOURSE

One of the most interesting features of Shakespeare's work
at this stage in his career, around 1595, is the tension
between the playwright's delight in rhetoric and his interest
in realistic characterisation. In his earliest plays, notably in
the *Henry VI* trilogy, a relatively formal versification often
tended to impede the capacity for individuated utterance. As
Shakespeare's skills evolved, as audiences became more
sophisticated through familiarity with standard conventions,
and as the tastes of the times changed, so characterisation
became more flexibly diversified in its modes of expression.
In the mature dramas, the tension between rhetoric and
realism is often so well resolved that we may, for much of
the time, overlook it; but it always remains, and, even in a
work as assured as *King Lear*, there are marked shifts
between speeches which seem predominantly the voice
of the given character and speeches which are relatively
impersonal. A characterisation is the product of a diversity
of claims on the writer's imagination: realistic mimesis;
furtherance of the plot or the thematic structure; interpretative comment; rhetorical display (oratorical patterning,
witty conceits, intensifying imagery); and convenience of
staging (for instance, a character may utter a rhyming
couplet to signal the end of a Scene or Act, there being no
drop-curtain on the customary stage). One sign of Shakespeare's evolution towards greater flexibility and away from
the constraints of formalism is, of course, the uneven but
marked reduction, between early and late plays, in the
number of rhymed and end-stopped lines; blank verse,
prose, enjambed lines, feminine endings, weak endings and
irregularities in the norm of iambic pentameter tend to
become more frequent.

In *Romeo and Juliet*, as we have noted, Shakespeare employs the familiar broad correlation between style and rank: lower-class characters are more likely to use prose than are the upper-class characters. Again, the poetry is predominantly blank verse, but (as is customary in plays of Shakespeare's early period) there is plenty of rhyming verse, now in couplets, now in alternating rhymes. This use of rhyme is sometimes highly functional, perhaps giving a deliberate element of the impersonal to the action: thus, when the Friar is speaking sententiously (as at ii.iii.5–26) the rhymes accentuate the impression that he is drawing on a stock of time-worn wisdom. The Prince speaks in rhyme when pronouncing grave justice (iii.i.190–9); here rhyme again 'abstracts' or partly impersonalises the character, for here he speaks as the voice of sage authority. Mercutio's utterances are exceptionally diversified (prose, blank verse, rhyming couplets and doggerel song) and this seems appropriate to his lively character. Frequently speakers move from blank verse to rhyme and back again with no greater or less justification than that Shakespeare, who enjoyed various kinds of music, would have it so.

In *Romeo and Juliet*, the characters sometimes speak very directly, as individual personalities, and sometimes speak less as individuals and more as voices lent various kinds of authority or degrees of impersonality by verse and particularly by rhyme. We may sense a tension between poetic description or rhetorical declamation and dramatic expressiveness. A related tension is that between a fecundity of wit and a diction appropriate to the situation. Occasionally characters move so markedly into a mode of wit that their utterances serve linguistic ingenuity rather than plausible characterisation: as when Juliet, though distraught, dextrously puns on 'Ay', 'I' and 'eye' (iii.ii.45–51). Often, however, the two are effectively reconciled: as when Capulet rather pompously and self-consciously compares Juliet's tears to a flood on which her body is a ship (iii.v.129–37) or when Romeo, on first seeing Juliet, says: 'Beauty too rich for use, for earth too dear.' In Romeo's statement, 'too rich

for use' connotes 'too splendid for mere utility' (with a hint
of 'mere sexual practice') and 'too opulent to need usury',
while 'for earth too dear' can mean (among other possibilities) 'too costly to be purchased on earth' and 'too endearing
for the world'. In the characterisation of Romeo, furthermore, Shakespeare makes some attempts to associate his
conspicuously 'literary' flights of rhetoric, like the definition of love at i.i.188–92, with an immaturity to be
outgrown.

Until chilled by fatality, the warm air of the fictional
Verona seems to induce linguistic intoxication: from Romeo
and Mercutio to the Nurse and Peter, all participate irrepressibly in witty language-games: a revelry of paronomasias
often seems, indeed, to be the natural condition of language
from which straightforward utterance is a self-denying
aberration. In moments of ease and relaxation, and sometimes even in moments of anguish, there are cascades of
puns, quibbles, innuendoes and exploited ambiguities. Even
the illiterate servant of Act 1 Scene 1 manages in his first few
lines of speech not only to parody the patterned rhetoric of
Lyly's *Euphues, the Anatomy of Wit* but also to exploit both
senses of 'yard' – 'tailor's three-foot measure' and 'penis'.

Samuel Johnson long ago complained of Shakespeare:

> A quibble, poor and barren as it is, gave him such delight,
> that he was content to purchase it, by the sacrifice of
> reason, propriety and truth. A quibble was to him the
> fatal Cleopatra for which he lost the world, and was
> content to lose it.[1]

In the 1590s, when Shakespeare was writing *Romeo and
Juliet*, John Donne was composing those *Songs and Sonets*
which were to make the Metaphysical mode, with its mock-
logic, puns and paradoxes, the dominant poetic mode for the
next sixty years. Then, at the Restoration and with the
burgeoning of Augustanism, came the reaction; linguistic
lucidity and ease were preferred to verbal gymnastics. Punning wit, which often exploits rapidly-changing vernacular

idioms, tends to sink into obscurity as the language evolves. So, from the late seventeenth century to the present day, the more ostentatiously or delphically witty passages of *Romeo and Juliet* have repeatedly been subject to cutting when the play is performed. At least the modern revival of interest in Metaphysical verse, coupled with the prominence of verbal gymnastics in such key Modernist texts as *Ulysses* and *Finnegans Wake*, has challenged the belief that punning wit is necessarily trivial or childish. An Elizabethan audience which could accept with ease the convention that a character might talk now in prose and now in rhyming couplets could also accept that an actor might speak now as credible character and now as licensed conjurer of verbal magic. The increasing recognition that realism is just one convention among many may encourage future audiences to regain the Elizabethan flexibility.

FOUR CHARACTERS

In this section, I select four characters (Juliet, Romeo, Capulet and the Nurse) in order to illustrate the play's dialectical qualities. First, some qualifications.

The attempt to isolate a number of characters for individual discussion entails a fruitful discomfort. If we examine the reasons for the discomfort, we promptly recognise the integrity of the play: its taut structure, the diverse ironies, its thematic coherence, its zestful orchestration of contrasting and interweaving tones and modes of discourse. Even very minor characters contribute importantly to the action: thus, at the opening of Act 1 Scene 1, the actions of Sampson and Gregory initiate the sequence of conflict which escalates, involving more and more people, until the Prince himself is brought to the scene to impose his majestically resonant edicts. Those two servants show how readily the atmosphere of the play can modulate from comedy to potential tragedy; they introduce us rapidly to the social world which threatens lovers; and they proclaim a theme and a problem, for they define masculinity in terms both of aggressive feuding and of aggressive sexuality. Again, if we seek the function of the exchange between the musicians and Peter at IV.v.96–141, we find many answers. The lines may, as some editors suggest, have been added to provide more work for Will Kemp, then the main comic actor with Shakespeare's company; but, if so, they well justify their keep. First, they continue to root the action in a credible social world. Second, they provide mutually reinforcing, mutually critical contrast. The lamentations of the socially high are contrasted with the insouciant grumbling and jesting of the socially low. The mundane practicalities of earning a living flatteringly accentuate, while yet placing in a partly-critical perspective, the raptures and poignancies of the lovers. And Peter and the musicians, as is so predictable in this fictional Verona, converse in punning wordplay. All the characters of *Romeo and Juliet* are participants not only in a tragic plot, and not only in a complex thematic evaluation of romantic love, but also in a demonstration of the ways in which language itself, fecund and protean, may be play, display, deceiver and truth-seeker.

Juliet

The boy-actors who originally performed such major Shakespearian female roles as Juliet, Cressida, Lady Macbeth and Cleopatra must have been consummately skilled. Cleopatra, fearing captivity in Rome, says:

> I shall see
> Some squeaking Cleopatra boy my greatness
> I'th' posture of a whore.[2]

The boy-actor who scornfully declaimed these lines must have been utterly persuasive as Cleopatra; otherwise, the reference to the squeaking boy would have invited the audience's derision. A problem for directors of *Romeo and Juliet* in modern times has repeatedly been that of finding an

actress who looks the right age (thirteen) but who yet has the
range and intelligence for this demanding role. By any
standards, whether of the Elizabethan era or of our own,
Juliet is precocious in emotional eloquence and dextrously
intelligent responsiveness.

   The first scene in which we meet her establishes, largely
by her reticence, Juliet's youthful innocence and apparent
docility. Her mother and the Nurse say much; Juliet
respectfully listens as the plans for her possible marriage to
Paris are unfolded; and her eventual response is an epigram-
matic model of dutiful prudence:

> I'll look to like, if looking liking move,
> But no more deep will I endart mine eye
> Than your consent gives strength to make it fly.

The obvious irony ensues: her next speech occurs in that
exchange with Romeo (I.v.92–109) in which, in the space of
a sonnet, she falls in love with the son of Montague.

> *Romeo.* If I profane with my unworthiest hand
>   This holy shrine, the gentle sin is this:
>   My lips, two blushing pilgrims, ready stand
>   To smooth that rough touch with a tender kiss.
> *Juliet.* Good pilgrim, you do wrong your hand too
>   much,
>   Which mannerly devotion shows in this;
>   For saints have hands that pilgrims' hands do touch,
>   And palm to palm is holy palmers' kiss.
> *Romeo.* Have not saints lips, and holy palmers too?
> *Juliet.* Ay, pilgrim, lips that they must use in prayer.
> *Romeo.* O then, dear saint, let lips do what hands do:
>   They pray: grant thou, lest faith turn to despair.
> *Juliet.* Saints do not move, though grant for prayer's
>   sake.
> *Romeo.* Then move not, while my prayer's effect I take.
>   [*He kisses her.*]
>   Thus from my lips, by thine, my sin is purg'd.

Juliet. Then have my lips the sin that they have took.
Romeo. Sin from my lips? O trespass sweetly urg'd.
     Give me my sin again.   [*He kisses her.*]
Juliet.   You kiss by th' book.[3]

The commentator who writes about this sequence may well
feel that he, too, is profaning with his unworthiest hand this
holy shrine; for the dialogue constitutes a justly renowned
epiphanic moment in literary history. The effect of the
context needs to be noted: the young lovers' words form an
intensely intimate, rapt exchange within the larger context
of feud and brawl, parental negotiation and bawdy chatter,
and within the more immediate contrasting circumstances
of the lively party with its communal festivity and its latent
danger. Immediately before the encounter of Romeo and
Juliet, Capulet has had difficulty in deterring Tybalt from
violence against Romeo; and the encounter is soon interrupted by the Nurse's summons to Juliet from her mother.
The effect of the poetic formalism of the dialogue is complex. When we read the play, it is relatively obvious to the
eye that the dialogue forms a perfect Shakespearian sonnet
and that the lovers follow it with the first quatrain of a
second sonnet before the interruption occurs; in the theatre,
the sonnet form may be less identifiable, but the formalism
of utterance and of exchange is still clearly audible. Romeo
seeks, first, to kiss her hand, and secondly to kiss her lips;
Juliet responds with witty circumspection, first warding
him off before making a poised concession ('Saints do not
move, though grant for prayer's sake'). Probably no lovers
in the world have ever, in reality, spoken as these lovers
speak, with such elegantly civilised, humorous yet earnest,
verbal dexterity. A familiar trope of the tradition of courtly
love and of the amatory sonnet sequence – lover is to lady as
pilgrim is to shrine or saint – is here given new vitality, for
this is a dialogue and not simply an address of male to
female. There is gentle humour in the amatory hyperbole as
well as wit in its complicated application to the immediate
situation; yet we may also sense that the religious imagery is

strangely appropriate, for, if it is hyperbolic, it is also the aptest language for the sacramental quality of the love-relationship which here is instantly initiated. Yet, from the perspective of common sense, there is additionally an almost comical quality in the extreme elaboration of the conceits; hence the aptness of Juliet's 'You kiss by th'book': that is, 'You kiss with the formality of an etiquette-book (and you sound like a sonnet-maker).' The formalism shimmers between sacramentalising intensification of the emotion and elegantly conceited counterpoint to it; furthermore, it is economically symbolic. That the lovers' first exchange is so poetically harmonious symbolises their immediate mutuality; it serves in lieu of many lines of conversation in which such mutuality might be more empirically and lengthily established. It certainly demonstrates that Juliet, for all her youth, is quickly intelligent and has an emotional responsiveness which is keen but urbane. Their exchange is both game and earnest; flirtatious and grave; wittily conceited yet devoutly reciprocal. Incidentally, by calling him 'pilgrim' (*romeo*), Juliet unwittingly identifies her masked suitor.

The shimmering quality of the play's rhymed utterances – shimmering between conspicuous and inconspicuous formalism – is emphasised again, a few lines later, when Juliet learns that the young man with whom she has spoken is 'Romeo, and a Montague'. She comments:

> My only love sprung from my only hate.
> Too early seen unknown, and known too late.
> Prodigious birth of love it is to me
> That I must love a loathèd enemy.

When the suspicious Nurse says 'What's this? What's this?', Juliet replies:

> A rhyme I learn'd even now
> Of one I danc'd withal.

'A rhyme'. In this play, rhymed verse can either be a

dramatic convention 'invisible' to the characters, being the dramatist's way of heightening discourse which in real life would be prose; or it can become 'visible' to them as rhymed verse indeed.

In Act 2 Scene 2, when Romeo in the orchard addresses Juliet on her balcony, it soon becomes clear that whereas his amatory mode is relatively conventional, uttering the hyperboles familiar from the long tradition of Petrarchan sonnets and romantic tales, Juliet's is more flexible, judicious and self-aware: self-critical and even astutely prompt to check Romeo's attempt to assert his love in conventional vows. In the following exchange, notice the way in which Romeo's lyricism is twice checked by her shrewdly intelligent distrust of, and impatience with, conventionally 'literary' love-addresses:

> *Romeo.* Lady, by yonder blessèd moon I vow,
>   That tips with silver all these fruit-tree tops—
> *Juliet.* O swear not by the moon, th'inconstant moon,
>   That monthly changes in her circled orb,
>   Lest that thy love prove likewise variable.
> *Romeo.* What shall I swear by?
> *Juliet.*   Do not swear at all.
>   Or, if thou wilt, swear by thy gracious self,
>   Which is the god of my idolatry,
>   And I'll believe thee.
> *Romeo.*   If my heart's dear love—
> *Juliet.* Well, do not swear. Although I joy in thee,
>   I have no joy of this contract tonight. . . . .

If she has forebodings about the outcome of their love, which seems 'too rash, too unadvis'd, too sudden', she yet can surpass all his poetical hyperboles with a majestic amatory paradox expressed in lucid clarity:

> My bounty is as boundless as the sea,
> My love as deep: the more I give to thee
> The more I have, for both are infinite.

And within a few lines, she, who had deplored the rash and sudden nature of their love-relationship, urges him to send word the next morning of the time and place of their wedding. This astonishing rapidity of momentum from their first encounter to their betrothal, a matter of minutes, might be explained (somewhat strainedly) on realistic grounds, given that Juliet is young, ardent, and aware of her parents' scheme to marry her to Paris; it is perhaps better explained by its harmony with the 'short time-scheme' convention which predominantly governs the action of this highly compressed drama, a convention to which we readily adapt. The play's opening scene has attuned us to the emotional impatience of this fictional society.

When Juliet meets Romeo at Friar Laurence's for the marriage, it is again she who checks Romeo's rhapsodic utterance by saying:

> Conceit more rich in matter than in words
> Brags of his substance, not of ornament

– though she immediately follows this with an affirmation which echoes the love-poetry of Ovid and anticipates the hyperboles of Antony and Cleopatra. Antony will say, 'There's beggary in the love that can be reckoned'; Juliet's anticipation of this is:

> They are but beggars that can count their worth,
> But my true love is grown to such excess
> I cannot sum up sum of half my wealth.

Later, at the opening of Act 3 Scene 2, burgeons one of the most splendidly memorable speeches in the whole of Shakespearian drama, the 'prothalamion' beginning:

> Gallop apace, you fiery-footed steeds,
> Towards Phoebus' lodging. . . . .

She welcomes with frank and lyrical ardour the onset of the

night in which her virginity will be readily lost. What is striking is that while the sexual eagerness is so pronounced, there is a marked absence of the merely appetitive or sensual; and even more marked is her conviction that the essence of the marriage is to be found not in the holy ceremony of wedlock but in the sexual consummation:

> Come, civil night, ...
> Hood my unmann'd blood, bating in my cheeks,
> With thy black mantle, till strange love grow bold,
> Think true love acted simple modesty. . . . .
> O, I have bought the mansion of a love
> But not possess'd it, and though I am sold,
> Not yet enjoy'd.

When Garrick revised the text, he cut out all these words except for 'O, I have bought the mansion of a love / But not possess'd it': Juliet's combination of innocence and sexual eagerness seemed too robust for prudish audiences. The lines have an ardent frankness in their anticipation of the loss of virginity in the sexual embrace as the incarnation of marital love; and the concreteness and precision of phrasing avert sentimentality and prurience alike.

During this speech, her ardour heightens to surrealism:

> Come gentle night, come loving black-brow'd night,
> Give me my Romeo; and when I shall die   21
> Take him and cut him out in little stars,
> And he will make the face of heaven so fine
> That all the world will be in love with night,
> And pay no worship to the garish sun.

There is something distinctly odd about 'when I shall die / Take him and cut him out in little stars'. Brian Gibbons offers this gloss:

> Juliet quibbles on *death* as also meaning sexual ecstasy: she prays that Romeo may share the experience with her,

in death like a rocket soaring up into the night sky and exploding into innumerable stars. . . . .[4]

Now it is certainly true that 'when I shall die' *could* mean 'when I experience sexual orgasm' (between the sixteenth and the eighteenth centuries this sense was often exploited by poets), but the notion of an exploding rocket is entirely Gibbons' and is not Shakespeare's. The lines might mean, 'If you, night, give me Romeo now, then in return I'll let you take him in the form of stars when eventually I (and he) are deceased.' Or, if we accept the sexual connotation of 'die', they might mean, 'If you, night, give me Romeo now, then, when I experience sexual orgasm, I'll repay you by letting you cut him up into bright stars to adorn your sky.' Either way, the association of ideas is odd. In the former case, there is the strange sense that when Juliet herself is dead, Romeo can then be translated to the heavens – even though *his* death has not been specified. In the latter case, there is the equally strange sense that when Juliet has experienced her own sexual fulfilment, Romeo can thereupon be translated – even though *his* fulfilment has not been mentioned. Gibbons says that 'she prays that Romeo may share the experience with her', but this is precisely what is lacking from the crucial lines, despite the fact that everything else in her long speech leads us to expect it. The basic poetic conceit is the bargain with night: if night gives Romeo to Juliet, Juliet will render him back to glorify night; he becomes the object of the fanciful transaction; and what jars is therefore the absence of mutuality and the brief sense that Romeo is disposable when not needed by Juliet. The Fourth Quarto shrewdly substituted 'hee' for 'I' at line 21; many readers may follow Garrick in preferring the resultant emendation, 'when he shall die', to 'when I shall die'.

Juliet's expectations of bliss are followed ironically by the news that Romeo has slain Tybalt and has been sentenced to exile. Her indignation at the killer of a kinsman is ornately expressed in a sequence of oxymora in an early Shakespearian mode (similar in style to Romeo's 'O brawling love, O loving hate' sequence):

Beautiful tyrant, fiend angelical,
Dove-feather'd raven, wolvish-ravening lamb! . . . . .

Here her indignation seems all too literary and ingeniously
rhetorical for modern tastes, which tend to equate conspicuous stylishness with insincerity; and a distrust of ostenta-
tious rhetoric is expressed by numerous Shakespearian
characters, including Juliet herself elsewhere in this play,
indicating that Shakespeare intermittently shared such modern misgivings. Juliet's subsequent lamentation over the
decree of banishment may seem excessive in its rhetoric,
given that Romeo is not far away and can soon be called to
her bedside. At least the point is made eloquently clear that
Juliet firmly and defiantly sets loyalty to husband above
loyalty to parents and kinsfolk. As the play progresses, so
the sense of Juliet's perilous and beleaguered isolation will
increase. After the parting from Romeo at dawn, there
follows the scene in which she incurs her father's fury
by rejecting Paris; she turns increasingly to Laurence for
guidance, finding that the Nurse is no longer trustworthy;
takes the potion after a vivid imagining of the potential
horrors of the charnel-house; and awakens there, only to
find that Romeo is dead. Even Laurence now flees in fear,
leaving Juliet to choose suicide and a reunion in death with
her husband.

Poison, I see, hath been his timeless end.
O churl. Drunk all, and left no friendly drop
To help me after? I will kiss thy lips.
Haply some poison yet doth hang on them
To make me die with a restorative.   [*She kisses him.*]
Thy lips are warm!
Watchman. [*Within.*] Lead, boy. Which way?
Juliet. Yea, noise? Then I'll be brief. O happy dagger.
This is thy sheath. There rust, and let me die.

The final lines have a terse power and poignancy, and they
gleam with mild paradox; the wit, though not obtrusive,

gives the sense of living intelligence to the decisive moment. The drop of poison would be a 'friendly' drop; on his lips it would be the 'restorative' (restoring her to him); and the dagger is 'happy'. 'Happy' there connotes (1) fortunate: by 'hap' or chance, she sees a means to die; (2) felicitous, bringer of happiness, since she seeks death and Romeo; and (3) happy in its role, since, like a phallus, it is to be thrust into her body; so 'let me die' may fleetingly invoke (again) the subordinate ironic sense, 'let me experience sexual bliss'. The First Quarto offers 'rest', where the later Quartos and F1 offer 'rust'; the reader may well deem 'rest' the superior reading, since it sustains better the covert notion of Death as lover and dagger as phallus.

If we look back over the characterisation, we see that though sometimes an overtly 'literary' rhetoric (particularly the sequences of oxymora) may have impeded the sense of personality in action, predominantly the impression is vivid and credible: Juliet oscillates between girlish fears and womanly maturity, preserving an adolescent fervour yet also, frequently, a quick and critical intelligence. She voices a romantic ardour which retains a quality of intense honesty, combined with a lucidity of utterance which protects the ardour from sentimentality.

Feminists may note that in a play which associates a pointless feud predominantly with masculine aggression, Juliet's emergent courage, strength of will, emotional and intellectual verve – indeed, her range of cogent articulacy – combine to challenge stereotypical notions of a youthful heroine. Her fame in literary history may have caused familiarity to veil her brightly original energy.

Romeo

In his movement towards independence from associates, Romeo's character-development resembles Juliet's; but, in his case, there is a marked callowness which he must overcome as he proceeds towards maturity. In his characterisation, as in hers, there is some tension between utterance that seems dramatically apt and utterance in which linguistic ingenuity draws attention towards itself; the rhetorical sometimes conflicts with the appropriately expressive. On the other hand, the conspicuously 'literary' features of his early devotion to Rosaline can be assimilated quite well to his character by arguing that the Romeo whom we first meet is 'in love with love', or, more precisely, is absorbed in an all-too-conventional role of the Petrarchan or courtly lover whose lady is disdainful.

> Love is a smoke made with the fume of sighs;
> Being purg'd, a fire sparkling in lovers' eyes;
> Being vex'd, a sea nourish'd with lovers' tears;
> What is it else? A madness most discreet,
> A choking gall, and a preserving sweet.

Here his relish in rehearsing the familiar paradoxes (familiar from countless sonnet-sequences) seems stronger than the woe he purports to be experiencing at his rejection by the chaste Rosaline. For a man who claims that 'in [her] vow / Do I live dead', there remains ample vitality in his entranced analysis of his lovelorn situation.

The later hyperboles of his addresses to Juliet as he stands in the orchard remain within the Petrarchan mode (the woman being seen as an angel, her eyes brighter than stars or sunlight) but gain a graver eloquence, sounding less like recitations and more like the expressions of lived experience. Because recent literary critics say much of ideology but little of beauty, it is worth pausing to relish the beauty of utterance in speeches like this (II.ii.26–32):

> O speak again bright angel, for thou art
> As glorious to this night, being o'er my head,
> As is a wingèd messenger of heaven
> Unto the white-upturnèd wondering eyes
> Of mortals that fall back to gaze on him
> When he bestrides the lazy-puffing clouds
> And sails upon the bosom of the air.

The Petrarchan hyperbole, in which the young woman is likened to an angel, is here lent new aptness by the fact that Romeo is on the ground looking up at Juliet who stands above him on the balcony. The lyricism is given unusual visual precision as Romeo imagines 'the white-upturnèd wondering eyes' of mortals marvelling at a heavenly messenger: the whites of their eyes would indeed become prominent as their pupils were directed above. The sense of the angel's altitude and variable modes of airborne flight gains fluent specificity in 'bestrides the lazy-puffing clouds' and 'sails upon the bosom of the air'. (The Arden editor prefers the Second Quarto's 'lazy puffing'; other readers may prefer Q1's 'lazy pacing', which is more fully assonantial.) The rich patterns of alliteration and assonance in Romeo's lines give them a fine linguistic sensuousness, and appropriately the seven lines comprise one long rhetorical arc.

As we have noted, the abruptness of his transference of allegiance from Rosaline to Juliet has its comic features which are exploited in his exchange with Laurence in Act 2 Scene 3. The element of callowness in his emotions is another feature emphasised by the Friar: at Act 3 Scene 3, Romeo's rhapsody of anguish at his banishment is so extreme as to make the audience thoroughly sympathetic to Laurence's rebukes ('Art thou a man?. . . . / Why rail'st thou on thy birth, the heaven and earth?'). Furthermore, that facility for paronomasia, which Shakespeare often over-indulges in plays of the period around 1595, results in the lame homonym of 'Flies may do this, but I from this must fly'; while the later half-punning enquiry, 'what says / My conceal'd lady to my cancell'd love?', is little better. The actor of Romeo is obliged to appear melodramatic and almost childishly histrionic at various points in this scene; not only at:

> then mightst thou tear thy hair
> And fall upon the ground as I do now,
> Taking the measure of an unmade grave[;]

but also when, at line 107, he attempts suicide. (There, according to the Q1 stage direction, '*He offers to ftab himfelfe, and the Nurfe fnatches the dagger away*'.) At least the effect of the near-hysteria of both Romeo here and Juliet at III.ii.121–6 is to enhance, by contrast, the mood of relatively calm and gratified mutuality at the *aubade* of III.v.1–25.

The sense that Romeo has rapidly gained maturity from experience is enforced strongly in Act 5 Scene 1, when he hears from Balthasar the false news of Juliet's death. When faced with this extreme crisis, he (as many commentators have noted) is no longer extravagantly emotionalistic and verbose; now the response is terse and decisive:

> Is it e'en so? Then I defy you, stars!
> Thou know'st my lodging. Get me ink and paper,
> And hire posthorses. I will hence tonight.

The visit to the Apothecary, too, displays a stronger, more soberly and morally reflective Romeo. The young man who had often seemed so obsessively absorbed in his love-relationships can now, even while seeking poison, take attentive and partly-compassionate interest in the impoverished vendor:

> Art thou so bare and full of wretchedness,
> And fear'st to die? Famine is in thy cheeks,
> Need and oppression starveth in thy eyes,
> Contempt and beggary hangs upon thy back.
> The world is not thy friend, nor the world's law;
> The world affords no law to make thee rich;
> Then be not poor, but break it, and take this.
> *Apoth.* My poverty, but not my will consents.
> *Romeo.* I pay thy poverty and not thy will. . . . .
> There is thy gold – worse poison to men's souls,
> Doing more murder in this loathsome world
> Than these poor compounds that thou mayst not sell.
> I sell thee poison, thou hast sold me none.

In these lines there is a brief foreshadowing not only of the satiric denunciation of gold in *Timon of Athens* (IV.iii.26–45, 384–95) but also, more importantly, of one of the most moving features of *King Lear*: the recognition by both Lear and Gloucester, during their suffering, of the neglected sufferings of the humblest of the poor.

Further evidence of Romeo's maturing is his subsequent exhortation to Paris, at the tomb, to desist from violence. Repeatedly Romeo, who had once been haughtily addressed as 'boy' by Tybalt, now justifiably addresses Paris as 'youth':

> Good gentle youth, tempt not a desperate man. . . . .
>   I beseech thee, youth,
> Put not another sin upon my head
> By urging me to fury.

Like his earlier exhortation to Tybalt to refrain from violence, this plea also proves unavailing; but Romeo retains magnanimity for his slain foe:

>   O, give me thy hand,
> One writ with me in sour misfortune's book.
> I'll bury thee in a triumphant grave.

The play's ironies are never keener than when Romeo, now seeing the supposedly dead Juliet, marvels at her retention of the beauty of the living:

>   O my love, my wife,
> Death that hath suck'd the honey of thy breath
> Hath had no power yet upon thy beauty.
> Thou art not conquer'd. Beauty's ensign yet
> Is crimson in thy lips and in thy cheeks,
> And Death's pale flag is not advancèd there.

The poetry is lucidly, memorably eloquent, and moves to a fine peroration which fuses the motif of Death as Juliet's

lover with the theme of 'inauspicious stars' and the running
analogy of lover's body to 'tempest-tossed' ship:

> Here, here will I remain
> With worms that are thy chambermaids. O here
> Will I set up my everlasting rest
> And shake the yoke of inauspicious stars
> From this world-wearied flesh. Eyes, look your last.
> Arms, take your last embrace! And lips, O you
> The doors of breath, seal with a righteous kiss
> A dateless bargain to engrossing Death.
> Come, bitter conduct, come unsavoury guide,
> Thou desperate pilot now at once run on
> The dashing rocks thy seasick weary bark.
> Here's to my love! [*He drinks.*] O true apothecary,
> Thy drugs are quick. Thus with a kiss I die.

If we seek the secrets of such eloquence, we find that the
speech is given connotative richness by its metaphoric
range; it gains sensuous memorability from the complex
patterning of rhythm, assonance and alliteration ('A dateless
bargain to engrossing Death', with its chiasmic symmetry of
'd', 'g' and 'n' sounds, being one of the more conspicuous
instances); and it gains a wiriness of intelligence from the
assimilated wordplay, as when 'quick' in the last line exploits three meanings, 'speedy', 'energetic' and (oxymoroni-
cally) 'vital, full of life'. What is thus completed is a poignant
and bitterly ironic tableau: Juliet, yet to awaken, lies in the
chamber of death, now accompanied by the corpses of her
lover and husband, Romeo, her suitor, Paris, and her cousin,
Tybalt; their youth mocked by the bones and skulls around
them.

The Nurse

The Nurse in *Romeo and Juliet* is a celebrated theatrical
'cameo role': what makes it a cameo is that though the part is
not a lengthy or dominating one, it is vivid, distinctive, and

provides an easy opportunity for a veteran actress to display engaging and even scene-stealing traits of character. The basis of the characterisation is ancient and even stereotypical: as early as Aeschylus' *Choephori* (458 BC) we encounter another Nurse who, vulgarly good-humoured amid the tragic action, is grumblingly ruminative about the infancy of her former charge and joins a plot against her master; while in Euripides' *Hippolytus* (428 BC), the Nurse is loyal, well-meaning, inquisitive, sympathetic and interfering, and her mundane, even reductive, outlook contrasts strongly with the intensity of the passion-smitten woman whom she serves. In *Romeo and Juliet*, however, the stereotype is given new vitality and memorability. Juliet's Nurse is strongly and boldly conceived by Shakespeare; from the first, when she appears in Act 1 Scene 3, it is clear that here the playwright is experimenting with realism of the kind that was to be further developed in a variety of ways in subsequent works, from the Gloucestershire scenes of *2 Henry IV* onwards.

The Nurse is presented as a widow of late middle age who already has the garrulity and reminiscential habits of the elderly (she is described as 'ancient', though a child of hers was born only thirteen years previously); she has served the Capulets so long that she expects to be sharer of Lady Capulet's secrets; she knows that her ramblings will be good-humouredly indulged; like other veteran servants, she delights in teasing those she serves; and she has a habit of complacent self-approval ('Nay I do bear a brain'). In Act 1 Scene 3, her digressive fluency and her precise recollection of domestic detail not only give her a distinctive realistic individuality; they also do much to create a credible past and credible social environment for Juliet. Shakespeare has learnt the cogency of the apparently digressive, the relevance of the seemingly irrelevant. 'Lammas Eve . . . . . wormwood to my dug . . . . . the dovehouse wall . . . . . Shake! quoth the dovehouse': the Nurse's recollections glance at numerous particulars which imply many others, invoking a wide social terrain anterior to the present action.

Her idioms, tending so often towards the vulgarly colloquial, make clear her social class and give a salting of
vernacular idiom to the verse. She uses credibly habitual
terms of endearment to Juliet ('lamb', 'ladybird', 'sweet-
heart'); takes a partly-prurient pride in Juliet's eligibility for
marriage; connives fully in the clandestine wedding which
would, if known, outrage her master; and is bold enough to
upbraid Capulet when he storms against the disobedient
Juliet (III.v.168–73). Her practical cynicism becomes overt
at III.v.212–25, when she urges Juliet to accept Paris as
husband:

> Then, since the case so stands as now it doth,
> I think it best you married with the County.
> O, he's a lovely gentleman.
> Romeo's a dishclout to him. . . . .
> I think you are happy in this second match,
> For it excels your first; or, if it did not,
> Your first is dead, or 'twere as good he were
> As living here and you no use of him.

From then on, Juliet pursues her own determined course,
the severance being completed at IV.iii.17–19:

> I'll call them back again to comfort me.
> – Nurse! – what should she do here?
> My dismal scene I needs must act alone.

Capulet

This is another strong cameo role, the outlines of the character being clear but with plenty of variety within the basic
parameters of the ageing, wilful, proud *paterfamilias*. The
character, in its semi-comic headstrong vigour, is established at once, when Capulet, hearing the brawl in the
streets, enters crying 'What noise is this? Give me my long
sword, ho!', and is promptly mocked by Lady Capulet: 'A
crutch, a crutch! Why call you for a sword?' (Old Montague

is similarly derided by *his* wife, making a symmetrical presentation and critique of the feud.) The long sword that Capulet seeks is already an out-of-date, unwieldy weapon in the era of rapiers. Decent but irascible, quick to wrath but capable of being chastened and humbled (both by the Prince at i.ii.1–3 and, far more powerfully, by the tragedy of the denouement); egoistically enjoying his power of hospitality, quick to join the excitements of the party; now considerate, now a domestic tyrant to his daughter: all this gives Capulet strong dramatic individuality. With the Nurse he shares that reminiscential facility which is often the hallmark of the elderly in Shakespearian drama and in real life:

> Welcome, gentlemen. I have seen the day
> That I have worn a visor and could tell
> A whispering tale in a fair lady's ear,
> Such as would please. 'Tis gone, 'tis gone, 'tis
>   gone. . . . .
> Nay sit, nay sit, good cousin Capulet,
> For you and I are past our dancing days.
> How long is't now since last yourself and I
> Were in a masque?
> *Cousin Cap.*   By'r Lady, thirty years.
> *Cap.* What, man, 'tis not so much, 'tis not so much.
> 'Tis since the nuptial of Lucentio,
> Come Pentecost as quickly as it will,
> Some five and twenty years: and then we masqu'd.
> *Cousin Cap.* 'Tis more, 'tis more, his son is elder, sir:
> His son is thirty.
> *Cap.*   Will you tell me that?
> His son was but a ward two years ago.

What gives a sense of realism to characterisation is often the inclusion of just this kind of apparently superfluous matter; matter which seems redundant in the plot, but which evokes familiar human characteristics: here, the pride in recollections (possibly inaccurate) of times past and of former vigour, and in the readiness to argue about associated trivia.

Even the repetitions (" 'Tis gone, 'tis gone, 'tis gone . . . . . 'tis not so much, 'tis not so much') evoke the familiar grace-notes of the speech of the aged, the verbal padding of vacuity and mental decline. Already Shakespeare is working towards the orchestration of reminiscential senility that is one of the strengths of *2 Henry IV*, as in the Shallow–Silence–Falstaff recollections of Jane Nightwork (III.ii.191–216), which in turn anticipate the tragicomic nostalgias which are a staple of the dramas of Chekhov.

One reason for the rich vigour of *Romeo and Juliet* is that the central ardours of the lovers contrast with, yet are given plausibility by, the attitudes of Capulet, the Nurse and others. The critical and enlivening relationships between the characterisations are illustrated by, for instance, Capulet's indignant mockery of the Juliet who defies his plan to marry her to Paris. If, to Romeo, Juliet is a saint, an angel, a messenger of heaven, the sun in the sky, to the indignant Capulet she is now a fool, a 'green-sickness carrion', a 'baggage', 'tallow-face' and a 'whining mammet'. Romeo's lyrical hyperboles meet symmetrical contrast in the vehement abuse. Shakespeare knew (as the Friar's words at II.vi.11–13 show) that the sweetest honey can prove cloying; so the sweetness of the play's romanticism is offset by the salt and vinegar of derogatory familiarity. Here Capulet's dramatic function resembles that of the Nurse. Against Juliet's ardent devotion to Romeo, the Nurse can offer her curtly dismissive comparison with Paris: 'Romeo's a dish-clout to him'. In such ways the characterisation provides mutually critical and richly creative contrasts.

· 5 ·

Sexual Politics

THE FAMILY AND MARRIAGE

When she marries Romeo, Juliet is thirteen (within a fort-
night of her fourteenth birthday): which, to modern audiences, may seem a bizarrely early age. Her eligibility for
marriage receives quite detailed discussion in the play.
Initially, Capulet seems reluctant to concede that she is
ready for Paris:

> Let two more summers wither in their pride
> Ere we may think her ripe to be a bride.

Paris counters with the observation: 'Younger than she are
happy mothers made'; to which Capulet retorts: 'And too
soon marr'd are those so early made'. Nevertheless, he
grants Paris his provisional consent, and only two days later
will be imperiously insistent on Juliet's speedy acquiescence.
Lady Capulet cites her own marital career as evidence
that Juliet is ripe and ready:

Well, think of marriage now. Younger than you
Here in Verona, ladies of esteem,
Are made already mothers. By my count
I was your mother much upon these years
That you are now a maid.

In Elizabethan England, the legal ages of consent were
twelve for a female and fourteen for a male; but, among
noble and wealthy families, marriages were often contracted
for younger children. Carroll Camden, in *The Elizabethan
Woman*, remarks:

> The age of fourteen seems to have been a popular one for
> the marriage of girls. . . . . Overbury's character of a true
> woman relates: 'Shee is *Marriageable* and Foureteene at
> once; and after shee doth not liue, but tarry.'[1]

Similarly, Camden points out, Jonson's *The Magnetick
Lady* suggests that fourteen is a ripe age for marriage. But
this was a matter of debate: Alexander Nicholas claimed that
fourteen was too early: dangerous births might ensue; and J.
L. Vives argued that women should be at least eighteen
before bearing children. Lawrence Stone, in *The Family, Sex
and Marriage*, demonstrates that the earlier marriages
tended to take place in the higher social strata, where
considerations of property and dynastic power often influenced the parents, whereas the later marriages were increasingly common lower in the social scale, where there was
little (if any) property at stake. He says that among the
wealthy classes in the late sixteenth century, the average age
at marriage for daughters was twenty, for sons twenty-two;
while among the middle class and lower classes the equivalent ages were around twenty-four and twenty-six respectively. Six per cent of the English peerage married at fifteen
or earlier. (In royal history, over the centuries, child brides
had not been unusual: in 1396 Richard II had married the
six-year-old Isabella of France; while Henry Bolingbroke,
who was to depose Richard and become King Henry IV,

had taken a bride who was no older than eleven, and who produced a baby within a year). It seems, then, that although a marriage at thirteen was certainly early, and a matter of debate among authorities, it would have been accepted as not unreasonable for a female child of the prosperous burgher class. In Shakespeare's *Pericles*, Marina marries at the age of fourteen; in *The Winter's Tale*, Perdita is about sixteen; and in *The Tempest*, Miranda is fifteen.

Lawrence Stone argues that, largely as a consequence of the rise of Protestantism with its polemical emphasis on the value of matrimony (in opposition to Catholicism, with its higher valuation of celibacy), there was an increasing, if still limited, recognition of the claims of the young person to an agreeable partner:

At first, in the early sixteenth century, children were bought and sold like cattle for breeding, and no-one thought that the parties concerned had any right to complain. But Protestant moral theology, with its stress on 'holy matrimony'[,] slowly forced a modification of this extreme position, which was only maintained in its pure state through the seventeenth century in the highest ranks of the aristocracy where the stakes of property and power were largest. To retain 'holy matrimony', which the theologians thought desirable in itself, as well being as [*sic*] a way to reduce adultery, it was necessary that the couple should be able to develop some affection for each other. It was therefore thought necessary to concede to the children the right of veto, the right to reject a spouse chosen by the parents[,] on the grounds that the antipathy aroused by a single interview was too great to permit the possibility of the future development of affection. This right of veto could only be used with caution and probably only once, or at most twice, while for women there was always the risk that its exercise might condemn them to spinsterhood, if their parents failed to provide another suitor.[2]

This account of the 'right of veto' tallies quite closely with what Shakespeare shows in *Romeo and Juliet*. Initially, Capulet tells Paris that he concedes to Juliet that privilege:

> But woo her, gentle Paris, get her heart,
> My will to her consent is but a part,
> And she agreed, within her scope of choice
> Lies my consent and fair according voice.

Of course, when Juliet exercises that right of veto, Capulet is infuriated and threatens to cast her out and disinherit her. Repeatedly in his plays, Shakespeare presents sympathetically the young people who seek to marry for love and in defiance of parental will. Valentine and Silvia in *Two Gentlemen of Verona*, Hermia and Lysander in *A Midsummer Night's Dream*, Jessica and Lorenzo in *The Merchant of Venice*, Anne Page and Fenton in *The Merry Wives of Windsor*: the pattern is consistent; so consistent and strong, indeed, as to call in question Lawrence Stone's claim that the parentally-arranged marriage was widely regarded as right and proper.

> The accepted wisdom of the age was that marriage based on personal selection, and thus inevitably influenced by such ephemeral factors as sexual attraction or romantic love, was if anything less likely to produce lasting happiness than one arranged by more prudent and more mature heads.[3]

Stone concedes that this 'accepted wisdom' was increasingly being challenged by the combination of cultural individualism and Protestantism's higher valuation of marriage and the guidance of personal conscience; but, if his main thesis were correct, one would expect Shakespeare's plays to present rather more sympathetically the assertive patriarch and rather less sympathetically the rebellious lovers. That such literary works may legitimately be regarded as sociological evidence is conceded by Stone when he discusses the fact that prosperous parents customarily handed their infants over to a wet-nurse for the first eighteen months of each infant's life.

> Only the children of the very rich, like Shakespeare's Juliet, enjoyed a wet-nurse who lived in the home and stayed on with them later as a nurse throughout their childhood. . . . . Sometimes the relation to the wet-nurse was the closest affinity in the child's life, especially when she was taken into the household and continued to live there after weaning. Shakespeare's Juliet was deeply attached to her nurse, but had only stiff and formal relations with her mother, who could not even remember her exact age.[4]

It is true that patriarchal choice of spouse may seem to bear authorial endorsement in *All's Well That Ends Well* and in *The Tempest*. In the former case, however, the King who orders Bertram to wed Helena is enforcing by his authority Helena's own free choice of partner; and eventually (if Bertram's tardy promise to love her 'ever ever dearly' is to be believed) this does become a match of mutual love. In the latter case, it is part of Prospero's scheme of reconciliation that Miranda should marry his former enemy's son, Ferdinand; but their falling in love is spontaneous and unconstrained by his will. Prospero observes:

> So glad of this as they I cannot be,
> Who are surpris'd with all; but my rejoicing
> At nothing can be more.[5]

In *Measure for Measure* the Duke does impose marriage on Mariana and Angelo and on Kate and Lucio; but in each case the marriage is desired by the woman and redresses treachery by the man. Fenton, in *The Merry Wives*, defending his clandestine spousal of Anne Page, presents a vigorous case for freedom of choice and against patriarchal control of marriage:

You would have married her, most shamefully,
Where there was no proportion held in love.
The truth is, she and I, long since contracted,
Are now so sure that nothing can dissolve us.
Th'offence is holy that she hath committed,
And this deceit loses the name of craft,
Or disobedience, or unduteous title;
Since therein she doth evitate and shun
A thousand irreligious cursèd hours,
Which forcèd marriage would have brought upon her.[6]

In short, the evidence of Shakespeare's plays is sufficiently
strong and substantial to call in question Lawrence Stone's
confidence that there was predominant acceptance of the
principle of arranged marriage. It looks as though there was
a stronger groundswell of sympathy for freedom of choice
than the sociologist's evidence registers. Ralph Houlbrooke's *The English Family 1450–1700* argues, indeed, that
Stone neglected evidence indicating 'a widespread belief
among would-be marriage partners that freedom of choice
was their right': young couples resisting familial pressure
frequently asserted that to deny the call of love was tanta-
mount to denying God's will.[7]

It seems clear that in the cultural shift towards a more
romantic and less proprietorial concept of marriage, Shakespeare's plays, so widely performed before so large a cross-
section of society, must have been significantly influential.
Germaine Greer comments:

> Shakespeare was giving form to the Protestant ideology
> of marriage, as it is movingly expressed in *The Golden
> Boke of Christian Matrimonye* (1542):
>> Let other set forth syngle lyvynge with so many
>> prayses . . . yet wyll I for evermore commend the state
>> of honourable wedlocke, which refuseth no kynde of
>> payne and trouble. . . . .
> The Protestant reformers believed with utter serious-
> ness that husbands and wives could and should help each

other to heaven; ill-assorted unions on the other hand were a dismal occasion of grave sin. . . . .

We have become so used to marriage as a central theme for serious literature that it is not easy for us to estimate Shakespeare's originality in developing the idea of the complementary couple as the linchpin of the social structure. The medieval Church regarded marriage as a second-rate condition. . . . .

Shakespeare . . . . . takes us through the whole development of a marriage relationship in a way that is profoundly original – it is because it has been so influential that it has come to seem to us utterly conventional.

. . . . . Shakespeare took up the cudgels on the side of the reformers, giving charm and life to their sometimes strident convictions. He projected the ideal of the monogamous heterosexual couple so luminously [in his writings] that they irradiate our notions of compatibility and co-operation between spouses to this day.[8]

Germaine Greer's view needs some qualification. Middle-class individualism (aided by the Humanist tradition) may have been more potent than those 'Protestant reformers'; and, in any case, the Protestant view was mixed and variable, and not always as progressive as she suggests. Official homilies for repetition in church, like the homily 'Against Disobedience and Wilful Rebellion', emphasised that as God rules the universe, so the monarch rules the state and the father should rule the family. Henry Smith, an influential Protestant, asked:

If children may not make other contracts without [parents'] good will, shall they contract marriage, which have nothing to maintain it after, unless they return to beg of them whom they scorned before?[9]

But these very qualifications help us to see that *Romeo and Juliet* is a far more radically – and radical – political work than it first appears to be. The politics of the play are no mere matter of a feud between rival clans. In the ages-long religious, cultural and political dispute between those different valuations of marriage which may be approximately, though with many exceptions, correlated with Catholic and Protestant outlooks, Shakespeare's sympathies lay rather with the higher valuation often attributed by the Protestant; and in the vast political dispute between the principle of the arranged marriage and the principle that young people should freely choose their partners on the basis of mutual love, he sides powerfully with the emergent modern preference for free choice and mutuality. He anticipated the radicalism of the 'Digger', Gerrard Winstanley: 'Every man and woman shall have the free liberty to marry whom they love.'[10] Given that in many parts of the world (among Muslim communities, for example) the arranged match is still the accepted norm, there is a continuing global struggle between relatively patriarchal and relatively individualistic conceptions of the politics of matrimony. In this struggle, Shakespeare's voice remains one which, among those who value liberal and democratic principles, commands respect and deserves gratitude.

A cynic might wish to add the postscript that since Romeo and Juliet are dead within a few days of their clandestine marriage, this play actually offers a rebuke to rebellious lovers. That is not, however, how their death is interpreted at the close of the drama. It is seen as a reproach to the intolerance of the rival patriarchs, and even to the Prince who had failed to curb that patriarchal power. Coppélia Kahn has argued that *Romeo and Juliet* 'cannot be viewed as a tragedy of character in the Aristotelian sense, in which the tragedy results because the hero and heroine fail to "love moderately"', for the primary tragic force is 'the feud as an extreme and peculiar expression of patriarchal society, which Shakespeare shows to be tragically self-destructive':

> Metaphorically, it devours them in the 'detestable maw' of the Capulets' monument, a symbol of the patriarchy's destructive power over its children.[11]

Yet patriarchy stands rebuked, and the play gives strong moral endorsement to Romeo and Juliet: their golden statues will endure side by side as symbols of a love which disregards the pride and prejudice of kin and clan.

ROMANTIC LOVE IN HISTORY

In *The Allegory of Love* (1936), C. S. Lewis offered a bold and provocative thesis:

> We are tempted to treat 'courtly love' as a mere episode in literary history – an episode that we have finished with . . . . . In fact, however, an unmistakable continuity connects the Provençal love song with the love poetry of the later Middle Ages, and thence, through Petrarch and many others, with that of the present day. If the thing at first escapes our notice, this is because we are so familiar with the erotic tradition of modern Europe that we mistake it for something natural and universal and therefore do not enquire into its origins. It seems to us natural that love should be the commonest theme of serious imaginative literature: but a glance at classical antiquity or at the Dark Ages at once shows us that what we took for 'nature' is really a special state of affairs, which will probably have an end, and which certainly had a beginning in eleventh-century Provence. It seems – or it seemed to us till lately – a natural thing that love (under certain conditions) should be regarded as a noble and ennobling passion: it is only if we imagine ourselves trying to explain this doctrine to Aristotle, Virgil, St. Paul, or the author of *Beowulf*, that we become aware how far from natural it is . . . . . French poets, in the eleventh century, discovered or invented, or were the first to express, that romantic species of passion which English poets were still writing about in the nineteenth. They effected a change which has left no corner of our ethics, our imagination, or our daily life untouched, and they

erected impassable barriers between us and the classical
past or the Oriental present. Compared with this revolu-
tion the Renaissance is a mere ripple on the surface of
literature.[12]

So, according to this thesis, romantic love, far from being
perennial and universal, first emerged in France in the
eleventh century, underwent various developments, became
widely influential, and may now be dying out.

The whole conception is now being attacked. Feminism
in politics, reviving asceticism in religion, animalism in
imaginative literature, and, above all, the discoveries of
the psycho-analysts, have undermined that monogamic
idealism about sex. . . . . [13]

Lewis was writing in the 1930s, and some of his references
now look somewhat out-of-date. When he spoke of 'reviving asceticism in religion', he may have been thinking of the
ascetic Anglo-Catholicism advocated by T. S. Eliot, and he
was certainly recalling (reductively) the novels of D. H.
Lawrence when he referred to 'animalism in imaginative
literature'. His references to the critical power of feminism
and psychoanalysis seem more cogent. Certainly feminists
have often (though not always) assailed the notion of
romantic love, regarding it as variously male-chauvinistic;
and Freud repeatedly depicted it as a mere sublimation of
essentially libidinal desire. Lewis, however, polemically
exaggerated the narrowness of the temporal and geographi-
cal limits of the love-ethic that he defined. Romantic love
can be traced back and abroad in numerous directions: to
the biblical *Song of Solomon*, to Plato's *Symposium*, and to
numerous ancient myths, legends and romances. As we have
seen, the sources of *Romeo and Juliet* include a first-century
novel by Xenophon of Ephesus.
  Lewis claimed that the French troubadours originated the
principles of courtly love which became widely influential
in the Middle Ages, became the staple of many later amatory

sonneteers, and provided the basis of the romantic conception of the ideal relationship between male and female. These
principles were that the desired woman should be depicted
as peerless in beauty and merit; that the male lover should
adore her and abase himself in various ways to win her sexual
favour; and that the relationship was necessarily adulterous.
Adultery was essential (said Lewis), because in feudal
societies marriage was 'purely utilitarian', and theologians
declared that marital love should be for procreation and
would be sinful if passionate and hedonistic. In fact, Lewis
was wrong to claim that courtly love was always, in the medieval period, adulterous. Sometimes it was, sometimes it was
not. When not, that might be because the lady remained
chaste in spite of all her admirer's blandishments, or because
the consummation was marital, or because the lady (though
compliant) was unmarried. Chaucer's *Troilus and Criseyde*
give elaborate expression to the code; but, though their love
is extra-marital, it is not adulterous, as Criseyde is a widow.
Again, Chaucer's *Boke of the Duchesse* elaborates the
principles, and the wooing described culminates in marriage.
His 'Franklin's Tale' also depicts marriage as the goal, as does
'The Knight's Tale'. Lewis exaggerated the significance of
Edmund Spenser as a writer who achieved a reconciliation of
the doctrine of courtly love with holy wedlock; Spenser had
many forerunners. What did matter, as we have previously
seen, is that Protestantism, the Humanist tradition and
middle-class individualism tended to place a higher valuation
than had Catholicism on mutual marital love, so marriage
could increasingly be seen as the goal of a passionate relationship. Spenser's *Amoretti* (1595) describes an arduous
courtship which eventually is rewarded when the lady grants
the lover her hand in marriage; the lady is called Elizabeth,
and it comes as no surprise for the reader to find that Spenser
did indeed marry a woman whose first name was Elizabeth.

Certainly some of the earlier influential sonnet-sequences
described an extra-marital love: most famously, the love of
Petrarch for his Laura. In *Romeo and Juliet* (II.iv.39–44),
Mercutio, seeing Romeo approaching, says:

Now is he for the numbers that Petrarch flowed in. Laura, to his lady, was a kitchen wench – marry, she had a better love to berhyme her – Dido a dowdy, Cleopatra a gypsy, Helen and Hero hildings and harlots, Thisbe a grey eye or so, but not to the purpose.

Petrarch had given new plangency and resonance to the courtly poets' adoration of the lady; and his sonnets served as a cultural intermediary between the medieval period and the Renaissance. His influence flowed on via numerous imitators, translators and adaptors: in England, they included Chaucer, Wyatt, Surrey, and the innumerable sonneteers who emerged in the 1580s and 1590s when there was a veritable craze for the writing of amatory sonnet-sequences; and the ardours and agonies of the courtly suitor were elaborated in such novels as Sidney's *Arcadia* and Lyly's *Euphues*.

One reason for the fluent ease with which Romeo rehearses (in 1.i.174–234) the woes and paradoxes of love is that they had already been uttered in countless literary works: 'cold fire, sick health', 'a fire sparkling in lovers' eyes', 'a sea nourish'd with lovers' tears', the unique and surpassing beauty of the woman, her merciless virtue, the living death of the hopeless suitor: all these had been rehearsed by Chaucer's Troilus, Sidney's Astrophil and many more literary lovers. Romeo's regret that Rosaline's chastity denies the transmission of her beauty to posterity seems to echo the arguments of the opening sonnets in Shakespeare's own sonnet-sequence (though there the poet had been urging a beautiful *male* to marry and procreate). In *Love's Labour's Lost* Shakespeare had both celebrated the craze for amatory sonneteering and criticised it in a variety of ways, exposing its self-indulgent features and emphasising that lovers' language should be a medium of communication rather than a mode of display. There Berowne concludes:

Henceforth my wooing mind shall be expressed
In russet yeas, and honest kersey noes.[14]

In *Romeo and Juliet*, Friar Laurence remarks of Romeo's infatuation with Rosaline, 'Thy love did read by rote that could not spell' (i. e. it was recitation rather than experience); and commentators have often noted that the relatively conventional hyperboles and postures of Romeo's desire for Rosaline give way increasingly, after his meeting with Juliet, to a more original and personal ardency of utterance. Even then, a central continuity with the courtly love tradition is provided by the sheer extremity of adoration of the young woman. That tradition had, with various degrees of blasphemous boldness, borrowed the language and procedures of religion for a predominantly secular and sexual end. The woman was so often declared a saint, an angel, a goddess, the radiant centre of all value, and accorded quasi-divine power to grant life or impose death; while the lover was her pilgrim, adorer, worshipper, seeking the benediction of a kiss, the 'grace' of affectionate approval, the heaven of sexual union. Although the more pious or circumspect sonneteers might defer to religious orthodoxy by treating the lady as an emblem of (or guide to) the divine, the broad tenor of this idolatry of the lady was often subversive of Christianity by its implication that emotions with the intensity and value of religious ardour could now be directed to a human object and an ultimately sexual bliss. 'Eternity was in our lips and eyes, bliss in our brow's bent', Cleopatra will say; and the infinity that matters to Romeo is the 'infinite' bounty and love promised by Juliet.

It is as though, to give realisation and expression to a growing sense of human emotional potential and of individual worth gauged by love, the language of religion had to be captured and redirected. C. S. Lewis may not greatly have exaggerated when he said that the effect of the courtly love tradition, in its evolution down the centuries, was revolutionary; it amounted to a sacramentalising of sexuality, an investing of human desire with the significance hitherto accorded to worship of God. What is evident is that this valuation of love is an aspect of that increasing sense of the value of individual selfhood which becomes prominent as economic individualism creates a generally enhanced sense both of human capacities and of the experiencing self as the centre of the known world. And in one obvious respect a play like *Romeo and Juliet* is far more progressive than any amatory sonnet-sequence, however admirably written; for, in the play, the responding woman has her own distinctive voice; her needs and ardours are not mediated by the male lover dramatised as the continuously-responsive recording consciousness. An American critic, Juliet Dusinberre, has claimed:

> Shakespeare metamorphosed the effect of the male cult of idolatry by making it reciprocal. . . . . Shared idolatry can grow into equality, as with Romeo and Juliet. . . . .[15]

Juliet, even more than Romeo, can be vocalist, lyricist and appraiser of their relationship; it is she, as we have seen, who curbs his oath-making conventionality; it is she who guides him to matrimony; and it is she who, dying after Romeo, is granted the theatrical accolade of the climactic death. Her role has dramatic centrality.

But how true to experience, at the time, was the depiction of the lovers? Lawrence Stone is predictably unromantic in his assessment:

> Until romanticism triumphed in the late eighteenth century, there was . . . . . a clear conflict of values between the idealization of love by some poets, playwrights and the authors of romances on the one hand, and its rejection as a form of imprudent folly and even madness by all theologians, moralists, authors of manuals of conduct, and parents and adults in general. Everyone knew about it, some experienced it, but only a minority of young courtiers made it a way of life, and even they did not necessarily regard it as a suitable basis for life-long marriage. . . . .
> To an Elizabethan audience the tragedy of Romeo and Juliet, like that of Othello, lay not so much in their ill-

starred romance as in the way they brought destruction upon themselves by violating the norms of the society in which they lived, which in the former case meant strict filial obedience and loyalty to the traditional friendships and enmities of the lineage. An Elizabethan courtier would be familiar enough with the bewitching passion of love to feel some sympathy with the young couple, but he would see clearly enough where duty lay.[16]

These comments on Shakespeare's plays would seem to imply that the bitter and racially-prejudiced Brabantio, whose daughter leaves him to marry a Moor, represents the moral centre of the tragedy *Othello*, and that the domineering Capulet of Act 3 Scene 5 of *Romeo and Juliet* is wiser than the chastened, forgiving Capulet of the play's close. The literary evidence strongly suggests that matters were considerably more complex than Stone claims. Some amatory sonnets may have been indulgent exercises in a literary fashion which did not impinge, in a practical way, on the poets' own conduct in courtship; yet Sidney's 'Stella' is identified in his *Astrophil and Stella* as Lady Rich, and Sidney was indeed in love with the Penelope Devereux who married Lord Rich; as we have noted, Spenser's love, in life, was the Elizabeth named in his *Amoretti* sequence. A relevant sociological factor is that in Shakespeare's day both church and state recognised as legal and binding a clandestine marriage lacking parental consent. John Donne famously declared himself, in terms of his career, 'undone' – because he had eloped with and married for love the niece of his employer's wife, causing his speedy dismissal by that employer, Sir Thomas Egerton. Stone notes that various young noblemen married in defiance of their relatives' plans, and sometimes were jailed or disinherited as a result; Houlbrooke observes that such marriages for love were more frequent than Stone concedes. Certainly, the pressures of family and clan, of business and trade, of convenience in work, must often have prevailed against romantic desires when partners in marriage were being chosen; but the very popularity, at all levels of society, of the literature of romance strongly suggests that the claims of personal ardour were increasingly being weighed against the claims of prudence and economic practicality. Among real-life courtships which were deeply romantic in nature, Houlbrooke mentions those of Sir Kenelm Digby, Sir Thomas Wentworth, Henry Oxinden, and Mary, Countess of Warwick; Lucy Hutchinson said that the story of her eventual husband's courtship of her would have made 'a true history of a more handsome management of love than the best romances describe'. Furthermore:

> Cases in the church courts reveal that passionate attachment was a common experience further down the social scale and suggest that the ideal of romantic love was deeply rooted in popular culture. . . . . In the seventeenth century, romantic passion and the thwarting of love matches were common causes of mental instability. . . . .[17]

In short, recent historical and sociological studies suggest that *Romeo and Juliet* may afford a more accurate insight into the cultural trends of Shakespeare's period than Lawrence Stone's work indicated; and they also vindicate the cultural force of a play which, at a time when the authority of parents (aided by those clerics who frowned on fleshly passions) was increasingly challenged by the inclinations of young lovers, sided strongly and influentially with the latter.

ROMANTIC LOVE: GRAND ILLUSION?

If we take account not only of the lovers' speeches, but also of the numerous bawdy jests in the play, the most important co-ordinating questions of *Romeo and Juliet* may seem to be these: Which is more valid, the reductive definition of love or the enhancive definition, or are both equally valid, or should both be seen as aspects of a fuller truth? Almost all of Shakespeare's plays contain bawdry. Bawdy jests, innuendoes, quibbles, puns, allusions. Given that while some slang terms endure, others are short-lived, there may well be even more bawdy allusions in Shakespeare than modern scholars can detect. Shakespeare is sometimes scatological, but his main preoccupation in the area of 'indecency' (as it has been termed) is with sexuality: with the sexual organs and sexual acts, with venereal disease and marital infidelity. *Romeo and Juliet* contains so much bawdy matter that the penis, variously masquerading as 'tool', 'weapon', 'tail', 'rope', 'yard', 'poperin pear' and 'prick', becomes a versatile performer. In a more puritanical era (the 1940s and early 1950s in England, for instance), the presence of such material might have been a cause of embarrassment to teachers and of furtive sniggering among pupils; in a more liberal or permissive era, it can be seen as integral with (1) Shakespeare's linguistic resourcefulness in general and (2) his analysis of the extent to which romantic love can be regarded as delusion rather than as truth – or, in psychoanalytic terms, of the extent to which such love is a mere sublimation of inhibited libido rather than an entry into a privileged region of specially exalted experience.

The source of the remarkable richness and verve of Shakespeare's finest poetry is also the source of his facility in bawdy wit: in both cases, his imagination is keenly responsive to the multiple associations of words; the root meanings, the ambiguities, the connotations: hence that mercurial linguistic vitality; hence the layered significances which close textual analysis so often reveals. In *Romeo and Juliet*, jests and puns which at first seem mere 'comic contrast' to the serious matter of the play prove to be all of a piece with the play's strenuous analysis of the various aspects and definitions of love. There are few modern theories of this topic which are not anticipated – with immensely entertaining verve – in the wit and 'indecencies' of the play.

Consider the opening exchange between Sampson and

Gregory, a sequence which now gratifies feminists keen to expose male chauvinism. Marilyn French rightly notes that the exchange reveals masculine aggressive sexuality (even if, confusingly and implausibly, she also suggests that punning humour is a distinctively feminine quality).[18]

Samp. . . . . I will take the wall of any man or maid of Montague's.

Greg. That shows thee a weak slave, for the weakest goes to the wall.

Samp. 'Tis true, and therefore women, being the weaker vessels, are ever thrust to the wall; therefore I will push Montague's men from the wall, and thrust his maids to the wall.

Greg. The quarrel is between our masters and us their men.

Samp. 'Tis all one. I will show myself a tyrant: when I have fought with the men I will be civil with the maids, I will cut off their heads.

Greg. The heads of the maids?

Samp. Ay, the heads of the maids, or their maidenheads; take it in what sense thou wilt.

Greg. They must take in sense that feel it.

Samp. Me they shall feel while I am able to stand, and 'tis known I am a pretty piece of flesh.

Greg. 'Tis well thou art not fish; if thou hadst, thou hadst been Poor John. Draw thy tool – here comes of the house of Montagues.

The ambiguities exploited here are obvious. 'Thrust to the wall' can mean 'push against the wall' or 'penetrate sexually while they have their backs to the wall' or 'penetrate sexually to the utmost'; 'heads' solicits the reference to maidenheads; 'sense' means both 'meaning' and 'feeling'; 'am able to stand' means 'remain alive and vigorous' and 'am capable of keeping my penis erect'; 'pretty piece of flesh' means 'attractive person' and 'notably virile, sexually well-endowed'; and 'Draw thy tool', meaning 'Draw your sword', plays on the bawdy meaning, 'Get out your penis'. Thematically, this all proves remarkably apt as an introduction to a play about feuds, fights and sexuality. Of course, the view of sexuality offered here is reductive: a mere matter of aggressive masculinity against women. (As Peter leeringly remarks later to the Nurse: 'I saw no man use you at his pleasure; if I had, my weapon should quickly have been out. I warrant you, I dare draw as soon as another man. . . . .') It also has a more sombre undercurrent, both in its suggestion that much sexual action by men towards women is a form of violence, and in its related suggestion that a partly sexual motive (the demonstration of virile force) is implicit in much violence directed by men against men. Shakespeare here anticipates, but subsequently challenges, Freud's assertion: 'Aggressiveness . . . . . forms the basis of every relation of affection and love. . . . .'[19] On several occasions, the play links continuance of the feud with those who take an aggressively reductive view of sexuality; and, in contrast, it links the ending of the feud partly with the authority of the Duke and partly with the romantic vision of Romeo and Juliet themselves. As we have seen, however, Romeo makes a fatal mistake when, in III.i.115–17, he prefers a violent, feud-based sense of masculinity to the pacific masculinity of the lover, deeming the latter 'effeminate'.

The play's bawdy jests generally imply or convey a reductive definition of the sexual: the implication is that love and marriage are cultural falsifications of what essentially is a quite simple matter of carnality. Lady Capulet's attempt to inform Juliet that Paris seeks her hand in marriage is interrupted by the Nurse's garrulous recollection of the time when Juliet fell on her face and then innocently replied 'Ay' when the Nurse's husband mockingly asked: 'Thou wilt fall backward when thou comest to age, / Wilt thou not, Jule?' And when the topic of marriage has eventually, and less indecently, been broached, the Nurse has the last word in the scene: 'Go, girl, seek happy nights to happy days.' Her implication is that that is what holy wedlock and marital love really come down to: 'falling backwards' by the woman; 'happy nights'; copulation.

The reductive view is maintained, with greater dexterity, by Mercutio. When Romeo is pining for love of Rosaline, Mercutio's remedy is simple: 'Prick love for pricking and you beat love down.' The superficial sense is: 'Stab Cupid in retaliation for the pain he has caused you, and you thereby defeat him.' The bawdy meaning is: 'Use your penis in sexual intercourse; you will thus punish love for having caused you the pains of frustrated desire, and you will vanquish it.' Mercutio's quite Freudian notion is that the anguish and ardour of love is based on sexual frustration; if you achieve sexual gratification, you elude love's claims; love is merely an expression (or sublimation) of frustrated lust. In Act 2 Scene 4, after Romeo has lyrically exchanged love's vows with Juliet, he joins Mercutio in an exuberant double-act of witty repartee, and Mercutio is delighted to find that Romeo seems to be cured of the melancholy of the lovelorn:

> Why, is not this better now than groaning for love? Now art thou sociable, now art thou Romeo; now art thou what thou art, by art as well as by nature. For this drivelling love is like a great natural that runs lolling up and down to hide his bauble in a hole.

The 'natural' he envisages is a 'natural fool' or congenital idiot who, bearing a phallic bauble like a jester's, seeks to hide it; thus, by analogy, a lover is no better than an idiot whose rhapsodies and yearnings are merely a delusive expression of his need to thrust his penis into the vagina.

Mercutio's reductive view has numerous echoes in Shakespeare. Sometimes other witty, worldly fellows echo it: Berowne, Benedick, Parolles, Lucio. Sometimes the speakers are sardonic cynics like Thersites. Sometimes a tragic protagonist, in bitter disillusionment, will echo it: Lear in derangement, Timon in the depths of misanthropy. Perhaps most significantly, it is Shakespeare's most dedicated cynic, Iago, inveterate enemy of love and harmony, who declares love to be a mere 'sect or scion' – an offshoot – of lust:

> But we have reason to cool our raging motions, our carnal stings, our unbitted lusts; whereof I take this that you call love to be a sect or scion.[20]

Iago is the father of a long line of philosophers and psychologists who have supported the reductive view. Bernard Mandeville, in *The Fable of the Bees* (1728), argued that love is a cultural adulteration or falsification of natural sexual lust:

> What we call Love then is not a Genuine, but an adulterated Appetite, or rather a Compound, a heap of several contradictory Passions blended in one. As it is a product of Nature warp'd by Custom and Education, so the true Origin and first Motive of it [i.e. lust], as I have hinted already, is stifled in well-bred People, and almost concealed from themselves. . . . .[21]

In the nineteenth and twentieth centuries, this analysis was strengthened by Freudianism, anthropology and Marxism. 'Even to-day', declared Freud in 1912, 'love, too, is in essence as animal as it ever was';[22] culture may refine and elaborate it, but at base it is appetitive, egoistic, and even incestuous. Furthermore, not frustration alone but also something in the very nature of sexuality decrees that there shall always be a 'mental absence of satisfaction': 'wherever natural barriers in the way of satisfaction have not sufficed, mankind has created conventional ones to enjoy love':[23] like Cressida, who knows that 'Men price the thing ungain'd more than it is',[24] Freud claims that both absence and barriers make the heart grow fonder. We recall that Rosaline was sworn to chastity, and that both she and Juliet were Capulets, so Romeo's ardour is related to 'barrier conditions'; indeed, he is constantly challenged by barriers: the forbidden feast, the orchard wall, the balcony, the sentence of exile, the iron gates of the tomb. Incidentally, Freud certainly experienced barriers, too: he spoke of his courtship of Martha Bernays as the 'hard times of fight and final victory':

> Then I had to fight for your love as I now have to for you, and I had to earn the one just as I now have to earn the other.[25]

Anthropological studies, in turn, have emphasised cultural relativism and the ideological inculcation of concepts of 'human nature':

> [N]either race nor common humanity can be held responsible for many of the forms which even such basic human emotions as love and fear and anger take under difficult social conditions.[26]

Margaret Mead reported sympathetically the sexual promiscuity of the Samoan islanders:

> Samoans rate romantic fidelity in terms of days or weeks at most and are inclined to scoff at tales of lifelong devotion. (They greeted the story of Romeo and Juliet with incredulous contempt.)[27]

Marxism claimed that romantic love, linked to matrimony, emerged as a consequence of the bourgeois economic system:

> By transforming all things into commodities, it dissolved all ancient traditional relations, and for inherited customs and historical rights it substituted purchase and sale, 'free' contract. . . . .
>   But the closing of contracts presupposes people who can freely dispose of their persons, actions and possessions, and who meet each other on equal terms.
>   . . . . In short, love marriage was proclaimed a human right. . . . .[28]

Nevertheless, said the Marxists, bourgeois marriage inevitably fetters love, (1) because of the economic dominance of the male, and (2) because the institution of 'holy wedlock' (designed to protect property) may bind partners when love has declined in one or both; therefore, only when property is abolished can mutual affection really flourish. Marxist scepticism was augmented during the late twentieth century by the structuralist and poststructuralist notion that reality is constituted by modes of discourse. This development is illustrated elegantly by David Lodge's ironic novel, *Nice Work* (1988), in the sequence when Victor, who holds 'bourgeois' notions of love, spends a night with Robyn, a Marxist-feminist lecturer:

> Ever the teacher, Robyn is, of course, trying to make a point, to demystify 'love'.
> 'I love you,' he says, kissing her throat, stroking her breasts, tracing the curve of her hip.
> 'No you don't, Vic.'
> 'I've been in love with you for weeks.'
> 'There's no such thing,' she says. 'It's a rhetorical device. It's a bourgeois fallacy.'
> 'Haven't you ever been in love, then?'
> 'When I was younger,' she says, 'I allowed myself to be constructed by the discourse of romantic love for a while, yes.'
> 'What the hell does that mean?'
> 'We aren't essences, Vic. We aren't unique individual essences existing prior to language. There is only language.'
> 'What about this?' he says, sliding his hand between her legs.
> 'Language and biology,' she says, opening her legs wider. 'Of course we have bodies, physical needs and appetites. . . . . But the discourse of romantic love pretends that your finger and my clitoris are extensions of two unique individual selves who need each other and only each other and cannot be happy without each other for ever and ever.'

'That's right,' says Vic. 'I love your silk cunt with my whole self, for ever and ever.'

'Silly,' she says, but smiles, not unmoved by this declaration.[29]

Yes, 'not unmoved by this declaration'. The irony of the sequence derives largely from the balance: Robyn may seem heartlessly intellectual in her 'explaining away' of love; yet she is capable of being moved, however vestigially, by his words. Vic maintains his romantic style, but he is an adulterer who here seeks immediate pleasure; and, in both cases, the discourse, whether academic or amatory, seems to be mildly mocked by the imperious dictates of bodily gratification.

The tensions which are so complexly developed by Shakespeare in *Romeo and Juliet* were starkly exploited by Aldous Huxley's brilliant satiric novel of 1932, *Brave New World*. There, John, the 'Savage' from a remote New Mexican reservation, is brought to the hedonistic society of a future England. John's notions of love and sex are based almost entirely on his repeated reading of Shakespeare's works (which, for the purposes of the satire, had conveniently found their way to his reservation); so his outlook conflicts directly with the ideology of the modern state which makes a religion of sexual promiscuity and which deems 'family values', constancy to one partner, and ardently romantic longings, to be obscene. John, falling in love with Lenina Crowne, expresses his feelings by reciting Romeo's speech, 'O, she doth teach the torches to burn bright. . . . .', and is appalled by what he sees as the debasement of humanity around him; whereas Lenina, conditioned to believe that only promiscuous copulation is respectable, is guiltily troubled by her persistent attraction to John. In an interview with Mustapha Mond, 'Controller' of Western Europe, John defends the value of human dignity and of the range of experience represented in Shakespeare's works. The Controller upholds the value of a docile, hygienic, harmonious society governed by the ideology of physical pleasure.

'We prefer to do things comfortably.'

'But I don't want comfort. I want God, I want poetry, I want real danger, I want freedom, I want goodness. I want sin.'

'In fact,' said Mustapha Mond, 'you're claiming the right to be unhappy.'

'All right, then,' said the Savage defiantly, 'I'm claiming the right to be unhappy.'

'Not to mention the right to grow old and ugly and impotent; the right to have syphilis and cancer; the right to have too little to eat; the right to be lousy; the right to live in constant apprehension of what may happen tomorrow. . . . .'

There was a long silence.

'I claim them all,' said the Savage at last.

Mustapha Mond shrugged his shoulders. 'You're welcome,' he said.[30]

On the one hand, the ideology of dignity, passion and idealism, with all the pains and sufferings which are their concomitants; on the other hand, the ideology of comfort and pleasure, without dignity, passion or idealism. And both, being ideologies, are imposed cultural shapings of human possibilities. Huxley's novel suggests that human values and human nature itself are always and inevitably matters of social conditioning, of political impositions, and possess virtually no bedrock of objectivity apart from the most elementary needs for nourishment, company, pleasure whether mental or carnal; the discontented idealist is seen as a social misfit. Huxley also suggests that the notion of the 'decentred self' is not necessarily liberating, since governing powers of one kind or another may exploit the opportunity to impose 'centres' or identities which may render the masses the more docile.

When we turn back to *Romeo and Juliet*, we see that one reason for its lack of sentimentality is that the text is so well salted with bawdry and with a reductive view of love which does contain a fair measure of common sense. For all his protestations of enduring love for Rosaline, Romeo will indeed be converted to love for Juliet within moments of glimpsing her. For all the lyricism of Romeo and Juliet, their consummation is a union in bed. Mercutio invites us to see romantic love as a fantasy developed by the imagination, encouraged by culturally influential writers (Petrarch and his kind), which only mystifies and rarefies what is centrally a simple matter of sexual frustration and gratification. Yet the contrast with the sceptical lewdness of Mercutio and the materialistic common sense of the Nurse makes the ardency of Romeo and Juliet all the more keen, poignant and impressive. Their mutual hyperboles of adoration, their fine lyrical eloquence, their total commitment to each other, and their eventual choice of death together rather than a life alone: all these are so memorably enhancive of sexuality as to make the explanations of Marxists and Freudians alike seem descendants of Mercutio's cynical bawdry and the Nurse's mundane practicality.

Historically, romantic love burgeoned at a time when religious modes of thought were still powerful but belief in God was being eroded by a new humanistic sense of the value of the individual; so religious terminology and religious aspirations were transferred to the exaltation of the desired partner. This cultural shift can certainly be explained in economic terms: as economic changes encouraged the free market and consumer choice, as materialistic demands prevailed against religious duties, so romantic love both celebrated the power of free choice and offered a private enclave of spiritualised emotion within the larger environment of commercialised appetite. Nevertheless, materialistic explanations of romantic love tend to be guilty of the genetic fallacy: they confuse the outcome with the genesis, as much as if one were to say that an oak tree is essentially only an acorn. Certainly the oak tree grows from the acorn, and could not have existed without it; yet that is not to deny the reality of the timber and foliage of the eventual tree. Culturally-suggested emotions may yet be real emotions. The cynic who derides romantic idealism may be sincere, but his cynicism may be no less culturally-conditioned and no more veridical than is the outlook of the idealist. 'Love is a madness', says Rosalind in *As You Like It*; and 'Men have died from time to time, and worms have eaten them, but not for love.'[31] Well, our newspapers tell us that sometimes disappointed or bereaved lovers do commit suicide; and, if love be a madness, it is often a more benign madness than, say, the power-hunger of martial politicians or the lethal bigotry of religious leaders who have advocated 'holy wars' of one kind or another. However much biological, cultural, social and economic factors have contributed to its generation, romantic love (in all its varying degrees and forms) remains a considerable and influential human reality as well as a much-propagated ideal. Shakespeare's plays suggest that one criterion of assessment may be this: love's reality is proportionate to the work and sacrifices the lover is prepared to do and make for the person loved. In *Romeo and Juliet*, emphasis falls on the sacrifice of life; in *The Tempest*, the labour criterion is cited when Ferdinand says: 'The mistress which I serve quickens what's dead, / And makes my labours pleasures.'[32] What might be termed 'the labour theory of amatory value', which specifies labour on behalf of another person as the most practical objective criterion of true love, is one which rightly concentrates on the altruistic and practical component; and it is this which we see so often in the love of parents for children and of devoted couples for each other. The memorable hyperboles by which Romeo and Juliet profess their mutual adoration both reflect and encourage a real if often muted tendency of human beings, at their best, to co-operate in the achievement of altruism which refutes the cynic and makes the sceptical materialist seem the victim of a reductive mystification.

John Milton, who wrote a paean of praise to marital bliss, also wrote tracts advocating easier divorce. Romantic love's enhancive conception of sexuality exalts some valuable human qualities; but it sometimes causes misery by setting standards of mutual ardour which are infrequently attained or are seldom durably met. The reductive view may seem more practical; but it often causes misery by its demeaning of human relationships. The sceptic who treats romantic love as an ideological imposition may forget that scepticism itself is no less an imposition of ideology. As Troilus remarks: 'What's aught, but as 'tis valued?'[33]

Conclusion

If thou art dun, we'll draw thee from the mire
Of – save your reverence – love, wherein thou stickest
Up to the ears.

Those are Mercutio's words to Romeo in Act 1 Scene 4. They illustrate the play's radical wit. 'Dun' is a homophone, linking 'done' (meaning finished) with 'dun' (meaning brown); Mercutio purports to see Romeo as a man enmired in love. 'Save your reverence' was a term of apology which customarily preceded some indecency (and is here used ironically to precede the word 'love'); but it was also, particularly in the contraction 'sirreverence', itself a euphemism for excrement: and Mercutio's syntax mischievously hints at 'excrement' as a synonym for 'love'. Repeatedly in *Romeo and Juliet* such reductive humour offsets the play's famed lyricism. This book has emphasised the dialectical, contrastive qualities which give *Romeo and Juliet* its tersely rich vigour: high comedy and bitter tragedy; sociable festivity, private raptures; violent hatred, pacific mutuality; expectant

117

youth, reminiscential age; marriage and funeral; the eagerness of vitality, the horrors of the charnel-house.

The previous chapter discussed the contrast between the
reductive and the enhancive views of sexuality. The play implies their interdependence. What gives comic cogency to the
reductive view is our recognition that the hyperboles of romantic love can be seen as a religiose mystification of merely
biological needs. What gives poignant cogency to the hyperboles is our recognition that the reductive view denies the
reality of altruistic emotional commitment. Each view derives energy from the other; each is largely provoked and
partly generated by its counterpart. The strong element of
asceticism within Christianity contributed to the denigration
of sexual desire; yet the religious advocacy of transcendence
of the temporal provided a powerful vocabulary to be captured by celebrants of romantic love. A fully secular era might
conceivably eliminate both the derogatory and the mystifica-
tory extremes of attitude; but, since sexual desire regularly
finds expression in a diversity of modes, ranging from the
brutal and casual to the exalted and noble, Shakespeare's
brilliantly paradoxical treatment of love in *Romeo and Juliet*
should remain cogent for many generations to come.

In the eighteenth and nineteenth centuries, productions
of the play commonly deleted the bawdy material; Shakespeare's critical intelligence was too robust for those times. In
the twentieth-century theatre, though the bawdy material
was often restored, the tradition of deleting passages of
conspicuously conceited wit was maintained; they seemed
to offend the taste for realism. Shakespeare himself was
aware of the tension between realistically expressive language and ingenious linguistic display; and, as we have seen,
this provides part of the play's dynamics. Modern audiences
probably sympathise with Friar Laurence's complaint,
'Riddling confession finds but riddling shrift', with Capulet's anger at 'Chopp'd logic', and with Juliet's warning:

Conceit more rich in matter than in words
Brags of his substance, not of ornament.

If present audiences, conditioned to value mimetic realism, are hostile to ostentatiously witty dramatic utterances, they may fail to appreciate one of the greatest dialectical challenges offered by the eloquence of *Romeo and Juliet*. The play, which in superbly heightened discourse both criticises and celebrates ingenious verbal wit, encounters reality most closely when it demonstrates how diversely reality is linguistically defined and apprehended. The greater the diversity of linguistic conventions, the greater the number of real experiences which thereby may be captured, epitomised, assessed, transmitted and emulated. *Romeo and Juliet* is a supreme drama of love: the love of life implicit in the love of language.

Notes

THE STAGE HISTORY (PP. xv–xxiii)

1. *Players of Shakespeare 2*, ed. Russell Jackson and Robert Smallwood (Cambridge: CUP, 1988), pp. 128–9.
2. John Downes, *Roscius Anglicanus* (London: Playford, 1708), p. 22.
3. Thomas Otway, *The History and Fall of Caius Marius*, p. 20, in *Five Restoration Theatrical Adaptations*, ed. Edward A. Langhans (New York and London: Garland, 1980).
4. *Romeo and Juliet . . . . . With Alterations, and an additional Scene: As it is Performed at the Theatre-Royal in Drury-Lane* (London: Tonson and Draper, 1750), p. 3.
5. Jill L. Levenson, *Shakespeare in Performance* (Manchester: Manchester University Press, 1987), pp. 31–40.
6. Quoted by Levenson, p. 54.
7. Jack J. Jorgens, *Shakespeare on Film* (Bloomington and London: Indiana University Press, 1977), p. 86.
8. Zdeněk Stříbrný, 'Shakespeare and *perestroika* in Prague', *Literature Matters*, No. 4 (April 1990), p. 4.

120

9. *Shakespeare Quarterly*, 39 (1988), pp. 798–806.
10. Sonnet 18; *Julius Caesar*, iii.i.112–14. (Wells and Taylor text.)

THE CRITICAL HISTORY (pp. xxiv–xxxii)

1. John Dryden, 'Defence of the Epilogue [of *The Conquest of Granada*, Part II]', in *The Works of John Dryden*, Vol. XI (Berkeley, Los Angeles, London: University of California Press, 1978), p. 215.
2. *Johnson on Shakespeare*, ed. Arthur Sherbo (New Haven and London: Yale University Press, 1968), Vol. II, pp. 957, 956.
3. *Shakespeare / The Critical Heritage / Volume 5 1765–1774*, ed. Brian Vickers (London, Henley and Boston: Routledge & Kegan Paul, 1979), pp. 434–5.
4. *Shakespeare Criticism / A Selection / 1623–1840*, ed. D. Nichol Smith (London: OUP, 1916), p. 42.
5. S. T. Coleridge, *Shakespearian Criticism*, ed. T. M. Raysor (London: Dent, 1960), Vol. I, p. 5; Vol. II, p. 99.
6. William Hazlitt, *Characters of Shakespear's Plays* (London: Dent, n. d.), pp. 104, 113.
7. Walter Raleigh, *Shakespeare* (London: Macmillan, 1907), p. 4.
8. A. C. Bradley, *Shakespearean Tragedy* [1904] (London: Macmillan, 1957), pp. xiv–xv, 12, 25.
9. H. B. Charlton, *Shakespearian Tragedy* (Cambridge: CUP, 1948), pp. 49–63; quotations from pp. 51 and 61.
10. Quoted in Martin Esslin, *Brecht: A Choice of Evils* (London: Mercury, 1965), p. 115.
11. Bertolt Brecht, *The Messingkauf Dialogues* (London: Methuen, 1965), p. 61.
12. D. A. Traversi, *An Approach to Shakespeare* (London and Glasgow: Sands, n. d.), p. 17.
13. H. Granville-Barker, *Prefaces to Shakespeare*, Vol. IV (London: Batsford, 1963), p. 69.

14. Caroline Spurgeon, *Shakespeare's Imagery and What It Tells Us* (London: CUP, 1965), p. 310.
15. M. M. Mahood, *Shakespeare's Wordplay* (London: Methuen, 1957), p. 72.
16. Harry Levin, 'Form and Formality in *Romeo and Juliet*', in *Shakespeare Quarterly*, 11 (1960), 3–11, and in *Twentieth Century Interpretations of Romeo and Juliet*, ed. Douglas Cole (Englewood Cliffs, NJ: Prentice-Hall, 1970), pp. 85–95.
17. Lisa Jardine, *Still Harping on Daughters* (Brighton: Harvester; Totowa, NJ: Barnes and Noble; 1983). Kathleen McLuskie, 'The Patriarchal Bard', in *Political Shakespeare*, ed. J. Dollimore and A. Sinfield (Manchester: Manchester University Press, 1985). Juliet Dusinberre, *Shakespeare and the Nature of Women* (London: Macmillan, 1975). Germaine Greer, *Shakespeare* (Oxford: OUP, 1986).
18. Coppélia Kahn, 'Coming of Age in Verona', in *The Woman's Part: Feminist Criticism of Shakespeare*, ed. C. Lenz, G. Greene and C. Neely (Urbana, Ill.: University of Illinois Press, 1983). Irene Dash, *Wooing, Wedding, and Power: Women in Shakespeare's Plays* (New York and Guildford: Columbia University Press, 1981); quotation from pp. 94–5.
19. See Cedric Watts: Chapter 1 of *Reconstructing Literature*, ed. Laurence Lerner (Oxford: Blackwell, 1983); section 3.81 of *William Shakespeare: 'Measure for Measure'* (Harmondsworth: Penguin, 1985); and Chapter 4, section vii, of the revised *Sphere History of Literature: English Drama to 1710*, ed. Christopher Ricks (London: Sphere Books, 1987).
20. Diogenes Laertius, *Lives of Eminent Philosophers*, tr. R. D. Hicks (London: Heinemann, 1925), Vol. II, p. 274.
21. Sonnet 111, lines 6–7.

CHAPTER 1 (pp. 1–12)

1. *Romeo and Juliet. Parallel Texts of the First Two Quartos*, ed. P. A. Daniel (London: Trübner, 1874), p. 2. Subsequent Quarto citations are from this edition.
2. See J. W. Lever, 'Shakespeare's French Fruits', in *Shakespeare Survey*, VI (1953), pp. 82–3.
3. *Romeo and Juliet. Parallel Texts*, pp. 88, 110, 148, 150.
4. William Shakespeare, *Romeo and Juliet*, ed. Brian Gibbons (London and New York: Methuen, 1980), p. 136. (Hereafter cited as Gibbons.)
5. This reading is one of many postulated and rejected in the past, but J. M. Glauser has persuaded me (in correspondence) of its cogency.
6. Ben Jonson, *Three Comedies*, ed. Michael Jamieson (Harmondsworth: Penguin, 1966), p. 113.
7. Hamlet, ii.ii.502, 543.

CHAPTER 2 (pp. 13–24).

1. Alan Sinfield, Chapter 9 of *Political Shakespeare*; Gary Taylor, *Reinventing Shakespeare* (London: Hogarth Press, 1990).
2. *Classical Literary Criticism*, tr. T. S. Dorsch (Harmondsworth: Penguin, 1965), p. 36.
3. Sir James Frazer, *The Golden Bough*, 2 Vols. (London: Macmillan, 1890).
4. This account of source-materials prior to Brooke's poem is based largely on Geoffrey Bullough's *Narrative and Dramatic Sources of Shakespeare*, Vol. I (London: Routledge & Kegan Paul; New York: Columbia University Press, 1964); Gibbons, pp. 32–6; and G. L. Schmeling: *Xenophon of Ephesus* (Boston: Hall, 1980).
5. Bullough, pp. 336–7.
6. Bullough, p. 303.
7. Bullough, pp. 284–5.
8. Gibbons, p. 42.

CHAPTER 3 (pp. 25–62)

1. *Hamlet*, ii.ii.401, 402–3.
2. *Troilus and Cressida*, v.ii.162–3.
3. *Troilus and Cressida*, i.iii.109–11, 119–24.
4. i.i.90–91.
5. iv.ii.1, 7–20.
6. Michael Riffaterre, *Semiotics of Poetry* (Bloomington and London: Indiana University Press, 1978), p. 12.
7. *Othello*, v.ii.361–5.
8. *Antony and Cleopatra*, iii.xi.65–8.
9. *The Oxford Companion to English Literature*, ed. Margaret Drabble (Oxford: OUP, 1985), pp. 843–4.
10. Thomas Rymer, *A Short View of Tragedy* (London: Baldwin, 1693), pp. 120–3.
11. In the first Act of *Love's Labour's Lost*, Armado begins his wooing of Jaquenetta; in the last Act, she is allegedly two months pregnant by him. Otherwise the play seems to span about two days. In *Measure for Measure*, the main events seem to take about five days at most; yet the duration of the Duke's absence is at least some weeks and possibly a month or more, since he is thought to have travelled as far as Poland, Rome or Russia, and has time to become well established as 'Friar Lodowick'.
12. H. Granville-Barker, p. 45.
13. Jonathan Dollimore, *Radical Tragedy* (Brighton: Harvester, 1984), pp. 89, 140.
14. H. B. Charlton, *Shakespearian Tragedy*, pp. 56–60.
15. Thomas Hardy, *Tess of the d'Urbervilles* (London: Macmillan, 1965), p. 446.
16. See 'Boece' (Chaucer's translation of Boethius) in *The Works of Geoffrey Chaucer*, ed. F. N. Robinson (London: OUP, 1957), pp. 319–84.
17. 'An Essay on Man', I, 289–92, in *The Poems of Alexander Pope*, ed. John Butt (London: Methuen, 1963), p. 515.

18. *The Works of Thomas Kyd*, ed. F. S. Boas (London: OUP, 1955), p. 164.
19. *The Works of Geoffrey Chaucer*, p. 331.
20. *The Works of Geoffrey Chaucer*, p. 189.
21. Bradley, p. 28.
22. *Julius Caesar*, i.ii.141–8; *The Tragedy of King Lear*, i.ii.116–30.
23. Spurgeon, p. 310.
24. Spurgeon, p. 312.

CHAPTER 4 (PP. 63–88)

1. *Johnson on Shakespeare*, Vol. I, p. 74.
2. *Antony and Cleopatra*, v.ii.215–17.
3. In line 3 of this quoted exchange, the phrase 'gentle sin' ('gentle finne' in Q1) may originally have been a printer's misreading of 'gentle salve' (meaning 'mild healing balm', with a pun on the Latin *salve*, meaning 'salutation'): see *Love's Labour's Lost*, iii.i.70–80.
4. Gibbons, p. 176.

CHAPTER 5 (PP. 89–116)

1. Carroll Camden, *The Elizabethan Woman* (New York: Appel, 1975), p. 93.
2. Lawrence Stone, *The Family, Sex and Marriage in England 1500–1800* (London: Weidenfeld & Nicolson, 1977), p. 190.
3. Stone, p. 181.
4. Stone, pp. 100, 106.
5. *The Tempest*, iii.i.93–5.
6. *The Merry Wives of Windsor*, v.v.213–22.
7. Ralph A. Houlbrooke, *The English Family* (London and New York: Longman, 1984), p. 71.
8. Germaine Greer, *Shakespeare* (Oxford: OUP, 1986), pp. 120, 121, 123, 124.

9. Quoted in Alan Sinfield, *Literature in Protestant England 1560–1660* (London and Canberra: Croom Helm, 1983), p. 70.
10. Quoted in Sinfield, p. 70.
11. Coppélia Kahn: 'Coming of Age in Verona', in *The Woman's Part*, ed. C. Lenz, G. Greene and C. Neely (Urbana, Ill.: University of Illinois Press, 1983), p. 172.
12. C. S. Lewis, *The Allegory of Love* (New York: OUP, 1958), pp. 3–4.
13. Lewis, p. 360.
14. *Love's Labour's Lost*, v.ii.412–13.
15. Dusinberre, pp. 156, 157.
16. Stone, pp. 181, 87.
17. Houlbrooke, p. 78.
18. Marilyn French, *Shakespeare's Division of Experience* (London: Cape, 1982), pp. 127–8, 331. (She says that '"feminine" language . . . . . undermines certitude and a linear view of experience through equivocation, pun, banter, and joke'.)
19. Sigmund Freud, *Civilization and Its Discontents* (London: Hogarth Press, 1963), p. 50.
20. *Othello*, i.iii.329–32.
21. Bernard Mandeville, *The Fable of the Bees*, ed. F. B. Kaye (London: OUP, 1924), Vol. I, p. 146.
22. Sigmund Freud, *Collected Papers*, Vol. IV (London: Hogarth Press, 1925), p. 215.
23. Freud, *Collected Papers*, Vol. IV, pp. 212–13.
24. *Troilus and Cressida*, i.ii.285.
25. Quoted in Ernest Jones, *The Life and Work of Sigmund Freud* (Harmondsworth: Penguin, 1964), p. 133.
26. Margaret Mead, *Coming of Age in Samoa* (Harmondsworth: Penguin, 1943), p. 11.
27. Mead, p. 94.
28. Karl Marx and Friedrich Engels, *Selected Works*, Vol. II (Moscow: Foreign Languages Publishing House, 1958), pp. 238, 239.
29. David Lodge, *Nice Work* (London: Penguin, 1989), pp. 292–3.

30. Aldous Huxley, *Brave New World* (London: Granada, 1977), p. 192.
31. *As You Like It*, iv.i.99–101.
32. *The Tempest*, iii.i.6–7.
33. *Troilus and Cressida*, ii.ii.51.

Select Bibliography

(I specify only those texts to which this book is most indebted.)

Anicius Boethius ['Boece'], *De Consolatione Philosophiæ*, tr. Geoffrey Chaucer, in *The Works of Geoffrey Chaucer*, ed. F. N. Robinson (London: OUP, 1957).

H. B. Charlton, *Shakespearian Tragedy* (Cambridge: CUP 1948).

Jonathan Dollimore, *Radical Tragedy* (Brighton: Harvester, 1984).

H. Granville-Barker, *Prefaces to Shakespeare*, Vol. IV (London: Batsford, 1963).

Ralph A. Houlbrooke, *The English Family* (London and New York: Longman, 1984).

Coppélia Kahn, 'Coming of Age in Verona', in *The Woman's Part: Feminist Criticism of Shakespeare*, ed. C. Lenz, G. Greene and C. Neely (Urbana, Ill.: University of Illinois Press, 1983).

Jill L. Levenson, *Shakespeare in Performance / Romeo and Juliet* (Manchester: Manchester University Press, 1987).

C. S. Lewis, *The Allegory of Love* (New York: OUP, 1958).

Narrative and Dramatic Sources of Shakespeare, Vol. I, ed. Geoffrey Bullough (London: Routledge & Kegan Paul; New York: Columbia University Press; 1964).

William Shakespeare, *The Complete Works*, ed. Stanley Wells and Gary Taylor (Oxford: OUP, 1988).

William Shakespeare, *Romeo and Juliet*, ed. Brian Gibbons (London and New York: Methuen, 1980).

William Shakespeare, *Romeo and Juliet* [adapted by David Garrick] (London: Tonson and Draper, 1750).

William Shakespeare, *Romeo and Juliet. Parallel Texts of the First Two Quartos*, ed. P. A. Daniel (London: Trübner, 1874).

Alan Sinfield, *Literature in Protestant England 1560–1660* (London and Canberra: Croom Helm; Totowa, N.J.: Barnes & Noble; 1983).

Caroline Spurgeon, *Shakespeare's Imagery and What It Tells Us* (London: CUP, 1965).

Lawrence Stone, *The Family, Sex and Marriage in England 1500–1800* (London: Weidenfeld & Nicolson, 1977).

Twentieth Century Interpretations of Romeo and Juliet, ed. Douglas Cole (Englewood Cliffs, N.J.: Prentice Hall, 1970).

Index

(Characters of *Romeo and Juliet* are listed individually in this main sequence; themes of the play are listed under the heading 'themes'.)